Your Hairy
Godmother

by
Michelle Casey

Your Hairy Godmother

Michelle Casey
HairCology LLC
P.O. Box 21305
Hilton Head Island
South Carolina 29925

www.yourhairygodmother.com

Ordering Information:
Quantity sales. Special discounts are available on quantity purchases by corporations, associations, and others. For details, contact the publisher at the address above.
Orders by U.S. trade bookstores and wholesalers. Please contact Michelle Casey through www.yourhairygodmother.com

Printed in the United States of America

Publisher's Cataloging-in-Publication data
Casey, Michelle.
Your Hairy Godmother / Michelle Casey

ISBN-13:978-0692553534
ISBN-10:0692553533

Interior Design by Mira Digital Printing

First Edition

Online Reviews and Client Testimonials

As a visitor to HHI from Canada I used internet reviews to choose a hairstylist to color and cut my hair. The positive reviews for Chez Michelle caught my eye and I visited the salon to book my appointment. After speaking with Michelle I felt confident in her ability to meet my needs. From the time I entered the salon for my color and cut appointment until the time I left Michelle made me feel right at home. She took time for a complete consultation before she began to match the color formula my own stylist had provided. I have to say that my color is perfect and my cut is outstanding. I left the salon wishing that I could take Michelle back to Toronto with me. I will definitely return next year!

Judi H. Aurora, Canada

My experience at Chez Michelle was by far the best experience I've ever had at a hair salon. From the moment I sat in Michelle's chair, and she began assessing the current state of my hair, and suggestions for the best possible options regarding color and cut... Not only did I leave my appointment absolutely thrilled with the way that my hair looked, I left with complete peace and happiness due to the incredible kindness and understanding that she blessed me with during my time at the salon. I am now a completely devoted client and fan of Chez Michelle! My expectations were exceeded beyond words!

Jennifer D. Hilton Head Island, SC

Loooved my visit here!! I happened to walk in right when Michelle had some free time between her appointments and she helped me out. I got my eyebrows done and a cut! I was very thankful for her help as I'd come to the salon after having recently been to a different one where I has left unsatisfied. Michelle and I talked the whole time about hair and more, she was very personable. She told me she got into the business because of her passion for hair. For her, it's not about the money, it's about the hair and it's about the customer. She told me her goal was to make sure each customer knew that while they were in her salon, they were special. And I'd have to say, from the moment I walked in, I was just that. I will DEFINITELY be back. I LOVED my hair, she made an awesome recovery from the former cut I had, it was perfect! She really knows what she's doing. Thanks Michelle =)

Crisee E. San Diego, CA

Michelle and Co. provide an absolutely fabulous experience every time. Michelle takes time to learn what cut works best for you - from the amazing shampoo and head massage to the final cut it's 5-star service every time! Guy's you'll love it here.

Bernie T. Hilton Head Island, SC

I love this place - Michelle really knows what she's doing and I always know I am going to come out looking better than I went in - no scary hairdo for me like other salons I have been to. Her clients are so much more than just a head in a chair - she really cares about making you look the best you can. I whole heartedly recommend this salon!

Julie T. Hilton Head Island, SC

One of the best salons I have been to. I took a chance being from out of town and it was so worth it. Michelle gave me great advice on color and cut. Wish I lived closer as she would definitely be my go to girl! My next vacation will be planned a round an appointment with Chez Michelle.

Joyce K. Gallatin, TN

Disclaimer

This book contains information about hairstyling relationships. The information is not advice, and should not be treated as such.

You must not rely on the information in the book as an alternative to counselling or medical advice from an appropriately qualified professional. If you have any specific questions about any medical or counselling matters, you should consult an appropriately qualified professional.

If you think you may be suffering from any medical or mental health condition, you should seek immediate medical attention. You should never delay seeking medical advice, disregard medical advice, or discontinue medical treatment because of information in the book.

Dedication

*For those who have taught me,
and for those who still wish to learn.*

Contents

Acknowledgements

This book could not have been written had it not been for the many relationships and life lessons I was blessed to receive. There are so many people who have unknowingly contributed to this book and given me insight and inspiration to write it. My intention was to bring awareness to others, when in fact, it has made me more aware.

My parents have passed on, but I still remember their words, and they continue to teach me from the heavens. I have recalled their laughter and wisdoms, taking refuge in our memories together during the hardest days. Without them I would not have seen the power in possibility. I wish to pass this great gift on to my children and grandchildren through the promise of this book. To my brother Mike and his family, thank you for understanding my recent absence, I look forward to spending more time with you soon.

There are few people in life that will travel the entire road on life's journey and stand by your side, no matter what. My friends, Jill Jones and Wendy Lee have known me from elementary school days in England, and still honor me with their continued love and encouragement. I treasure our Trans-Atlantic chats and visits. You're the best!

Thanks to cousins Paula and RA Green who called us to America and supported my family through the transition. My life on American soil sprouted a new flower garden of friends and they have continued to bloom for decades. Dawnne Donovan without you I would have doubted myself as a speaker. Thank you for believing in me and guiding me through my first opportunity. Bob Kilbourne and Julie Gillam, without you I couldn't have gotten through my days as a single mom. Thanks to Teresa Hendrix and Connie Rinaldi whose kind hearts could never be appreciated enough. Major Mike Casavant, thanks for gently tugging at my shirt and reminding me not to miss the best sunrises and sunsets, as well as keeping me sane when the writing became so overwhelming.

Special thanks to Lynn Renn who's friendship in beauty school transcended and blossomed in to a life-long bond. Our daily phone calls inspire me and give me clarity. The 25 years filled with hours of conversation shared have been key factors in the development of this book, as we worked through so many things together, sorting out the problems in our world.

My life in Hilton Head would not have been a success without Joanne Gamilis who connected me to Avis Rollsion from the Porcupine and Bev Martin from Tara's. These three women put me on the map of Hilton-Head Island and without them I would be telling a different story.

N.A.M.I (National Alliance for Mental Illness) was also a crucial component in this process. Many thanks Debbie Morris, Dr. Deby Lynes and to Marti Bloch who inspired me to teach the Family to Family program.

The Napoleon Hill foundation and fellow Certified Leaders are instrumental in the action plan of this book by applying the 17 Principles of achievement. Ann McNeill, Dawn Fobbs and Havilah Molone pointed the way for me. Thanks also to Judy Williamson and Uriel "Chino" Martinez for their leadership and support.

Also thank you to Toastmasters HHI and Elizabeth Millen from Pink Magazine.

John Paul Mitchell Education was a major turning point in my career and I still believe in their "Giving Back is the New Black." My educator friends with whom I certified are so precious and inspire me. Jenelle Gordon, Todd and Suzy Tryall, Cara Hodges, Sarah Hayle and April Roberts. What an amazing experience we had with mentors Jadie Solomon, Ladonna Dryer, Roger Cribb and Judith Moore.

Anna Troxler guided me through the training and directed the way with Paul Mitchell and still mentors me today. Thank you for challenging me and inspiring me to be better.

Finally, I can't express enough gratitude to my staff and clients. Catie Wolfe and Leslie Harris have been my rocks during the toughest times in recent years. Thank you for helping me laugh through the tears, as we built our salon castle together, and smiling with me now as we plan our adventures beyond the castle walls.

Note to the Reader

Your Hairy Godmother is your very own hair trauma preventionist. She, or he, is the person you trust most while seated in the salon chair. This mystical person takes the *mis*— out of *miscommunications* in the salon environment, preventing hair horrors for you and your loved ones.

Have you ever left a salon and said to yourself, "This is not what I asked for; I hate it," or, "They did it to me again!" Why won't these stylists listen?

I feel certain that if it hasn't happened to you, then it's happened to someone you know. This is such a common occurrence that it is practically an epidemic in the salon environment. Consequently, this book has been written to help those frustrated people leaving the salon, as well as those who stand diligently on the other side of the chair. It's time to start the conversation on how to prevent these common occurrences. Join forces in learning the *real secrets* to avoiding bad hair days and hair trauma.

This book was inspired by the clients that I have loved, lost and disappointed over the past 26 years. In essence, these clients have written this book with me, because the words I heard then, or perhaps didn't understand then, speak to me now in hindsight.

For those I've let down along the way, this is my humble apology.

For those that I have met, and learned from, this is my heartfelt thank you letter.

Finally, for those clients who have loved me in spite of my flaws, and who have suffered with me while I've grown, remaining patient and loyal through the hardest of times; this is an expression of my eternal gratitude to you.

It is my sincere hope that after reading this book, a new awareness will emerge to improve communications both in and out of the salon. I believe it will help us recognize our connection to the problem, as well as identify ways to resolve it. At the very least, I hope to start a national conversation and bring a new focus to one of the many causes of salon mishaps. I offer solutions as a means of neutralizing the symptomatic issues and complaints that have proven futile up until this point.

Your Hairy Godmother is a gender-neutral person in concept, as well as *your* perfect hairstylist. This person is someone who understands your needs in the salon, and who can identify and deliver the consistent results you want. These needs are unique and personal to each and every salon guest.

I have opted primarily to reference the female gender in this book, purely as a means of creative expression. It was easier to maintain the flow of the book without the constant repetition of *he or she*, and *him or her*.

Similarly, as a specialist in women's hair care my general references to female clients are the result of my experience. I have been privileged to serve many male salon guests, but the majority of my business is indeed female.

I hope that as you read this book, you'll keep an open mind while laughing and learning your way to a deeper appreciation of both yourself and your stylist. My goal is for new wisdoms and inspirations to bring you closer to Your Hairy Godmother.

Chapter 1

Once Upon A Time...

Once upon a time, there was a princess who had a wish. She wished that she could find a place where someone would listen to her and dress her hair the way *she* liked! Her dream was to be able to go to any ball, live in any castle, with or without her wonderful prince, and feel confident each time she looked in her mirror.

This modern-day princess does not resemble the characters typecast in old animated movies. She is passionate, loving and does not necessarily need a man to complete her story. She is her own woman, enjoying her independence and free will in a limitless world of possibilities. Yet, with the demands of her kingdom, the princess still experiences self-doubt from time to time.

There is no fairy godmother she can call upon in these modern times, but she can indeed find her own "Hairy" Godmother. However, she must be patient as she searches far and wide. On this journey, she will learn new wisdoms, discover a magic like no other and unlock the power within herself to realize her dreams.

Do dreams really come true? Wouldn't it be wonderful if someone could just wave a magic wand and make it all happen? Do you believe that you can find your

"Hairy" Godmother? Who is she? Where is she? And is there any *real* magic in that wand?

Yes, there is real magic! I know it's really there, because I have experienced it and shared it with others. People may have a hard time believing in it, as the perception of magic is often misunderstood.

You see, the *real* magic is in *how* we connect, and in those with *whom* we choose to connect. Hair curses are not the fault of the magic wand. Rather, the troubles more likely stem from the misinterpretation of words shared between the princess and her hairdresser. The main culprits are miscommunication and perception. Do you remember the wobbly spells of Aunt Clara and Aunt Esmeralda from the old sitcom series *Bewitched*? Even though their intentions were good, mayhem would strike each time they misspoke the words of their spells.

Your Hairy Godmother will correct any misspoken spells in salons. She knows all the right words in order to empower you while you are seated in the salon chair. Your Hairy Godmother is your perfect stylist and can be as hard to find as the perfect prince or princess. She exists, and is waiting just for you!

Do you still believe in fairytales, and in the idea that there is somebody special out there for each and every one of us? Could it really be just a bunch of hocus pocus? I think not!

As a hairdresser and a business owner, and after 26 years in the salon industry, I've learned volumes from my own communication mishaps. I recognized certain similarities in my personal and professional relationships, which I connected to the power of perception. The confusion that stems from assumptions and preconceived ideas, quite often, is a major obstacle that keeps us from communicating clearly. Feelings may become elevated and defensive, making it difficult to resolve even the simplest things. When perceptions and expectations are not managed correctly, this creates a breeding ground for polarized views and frustration. Despite hard lessons and disappointments, I must declare that I still believe in the magic of salon chair miracles. Yes, I'll even say it again...I believe!

Magic begins in salon consultations, and is powered with effective communication. Despite their best intentions, both clients and stylists have been caught in the snares of misunderstanding.

The three most common communication problems encountered by salon clients are:

1. Not knowing what to ask for—No clear guidance to make empowered, informed decisions

2. Not getting what they asked for—Not being heard or responded to correctly

3. Not getting what they *thought* they asked for—Not understanding their service choice

Stylists should feel empowered by helpful communications skills and techniques. Here are three objectives a stylist must master in order to communicate effectively and identify the client's basic needs:

1. The client's highest priority—Understand the
   level of importance and the *why* factor

2. The client's best option—Offer solutions
   acknowledging the client's priority

3. Translation of benefits and ramifications of
   options available—Empower the client

Confusing communication is an epidemic that affects
both sides of the salon chair. At times, it may cause
frustrations to linger and go unresolved.

As a veteran hairstylist and a Certified Professional Life
Coach, I have realized that for the most part, we are
all trying to do our best, in our own way. Most people
want to feel connected, but what they really need is to
experience connection in a way that makes them feel
safe while their individual needs are understood by
everyone involved.

Isn't it logical that if we don't know what we want, or
if we don't know how to ask for it effectively, then we
are destined to struggle with our happiness? Happiness
is found in the certainty of knowing what we want and
in the belief that we can have it. It really is that simple,
and yet many people are missing the *real magic* here!

Why don't we ask for what we want? Some people feel
intimidated, or they may be concerned about feeling
like a nuisance. Others worry about causing conflict
or hostility. If the words come out wrong, or if they
misstep in some way, the situation could worsen, and
leave them feeling guilty and ashamed. Blame is the
standard open ended outcome, and is counterproductive
to the original idea.

Oftentimes, the problem is rooted in the inner critic. I have observed thousands of people staring at their reflections in the mirror, and expressing their feelings of inadequacy, or that they are "never enough." Many fail to see the magic in their own reflection, which can allow negativity to permeate their daily lives. For these people, their own inner critic is the voice that they hear more often than any other. I can hear their echoes, as they are reflected in the salon mirror.

A couple of years ago, I read *Daring Greatly* by Dr. Brene Brown. I had an epiphany as Dr. Brown confirmed my own thoughts and experiences, as she described the "Never Enough Culture" that we live in. Dr. Brown's research was based on more than a decade of documented interviews with over 10,000 people from all walks of life, and their shared feelings of vulnerability. My records show that I have had at least 8,000 conversations in my salon since 2010; I've witnessed enough vulnerability to know for a fact that Dr. Brown's research is spot on.

This brings me to why I decided to write this book. It is in part for those poor unfortunate souls who have suffered personal horrors while sitting in the salon chair, and for those stunned stylists standing behind them, holding the smoking gun, and feeling responsible for every bad thing that happened. I will mention here that I have been on both sides of that situation, which is why I am so passionate about this topic.

Hairdressers and Their Dungeons

Are you one of those clients who feels stuck in the dungeons of a bad hairdresser relationship? Are you afraid to cut ties, even though you hold the keys? I will share new insights for you to consider.

In addition, I will address those who prefer to live on the other side of the client spectrum, known to us in the industry as "chair-hoppers." Their focus is on convenience and acceptable service. In other words, they prefer to avoid the hassle of time constraints and complicated commitments to stylists and salons. These busy clients often have more important priorities to consider than hair appointments, and so they operate like an elite special force. They seem to appear out of nowhere– they get in, get out and are gone.

In my experience, men are more likely to be found in this category. However, these days, it's not just the guys; ladies are very busy too. These "on-the-go" clients are willing to take a chance and venture into unfamiliar settings, in exchange for convenience. This may increase their risk for an unpleasant salon experience or disappointing outcome. And yet, these are tough and resilient clients who have learned to master the ropes. I salute and respect these clients. However, sometimes there's no place like home. Wouldn't it be great if someone knew exactly what you wanted, without any need to repeat it over and over again to strangers? Having a go-to stylist has many advantages.

I will not, of course, forsake those people who continue to hold out hope for miracles in the salon. These troopers keep plodding along through the frustrating terrain of salon relationships, trying to maintain a positive attitude, only to experience even more disappointment and mistrust. It can, and will, get better. Hang in there! Keep reading!

If you are one of the few to have been blessed enough to find your very own Hairy Godmother, there may still be a place somewhere in the dark recesses of your mind, where fear lingers in knowing that your stylist may not always be available. You may lose her through the cares of life, and its ever-changing twists and turns. Don't worry. I have a few ideas that may help.

Stylists face a different set of fears and have developed their own coping strategies. I, for example, rely on humor. Humor is good for everyone, as long as it's not at the expense of someone else's feelings. The humor I use in this book is not intended to hurt anyone. Rather, I hope that it will help us learn to laugh at things a little more.

Hairdressers have joked for years, saying, "It's a comb not a wand!" This response emerged in the industry through seemingly unrealistic requests by hair clients. Clients have eagerly arrived, clinging to treasured images of possible ideas for their illustrious locks, only to be met with mockery and ridicule when in the styling chair. Some may witness the dismay of their head-shaking stylist who is mentally scrambling for the right words to say. In the end, both hairdressers and clients are too often saying the same thing: "They just won't listen!"

We must stop the madness!

An apathetic stylist with a "been there, done that" attitude can make salon appointments very uncomfortable, and even intimidating for some. Clients who sit in these salon chairs may feel brushed off or ignored. And these stylists, who may have become emotionally callused while coping with the demands of the industry, have lost their sense of compassion. I believe the root cause is the result of a lack of hope or inspiration, as well as submission to the status quo.

To those stylists who are struggling with burnout, I recommend shifting your focus back to growth and creativity. It is wise to remember that the stage following *fully ripe* is *rot*. Clients may even witness the talents of this stylist at work, and believe they are in good hands, but that is precisely when disaster strikes. Ironically, gifted stylists are often guilty of the biggest violations of trust against those who occupy their salon chair. Careless communication can cause long-term negative effects for both clients and stylists.

Again, we must stop the madness!

I feel so badly for those poor hair trauma victims, for those who are scarred by haircut butchery from the inexperienced stylist, as well as for those clients who have suffered from salon chemical and color casualties. Some ladies, after a severe enough salon trauma, are left feeling like there is no other option but to lean on the support of their beloved husbands and friends, who woefully attempt to navigate the unfamiliar tundra of the "box color world." This legion of clients bravely continue to hold their own in the trenches of household kitchens and bathrooms across the nation. I am here to help you too.

A Little Word for the King and His Castle

Don't be discouraged, men. I have set aside a chapter just for you. Dr. John Gray says, "Men are from Mars, Women are from Venus." You may skip all of the *girly* stuff, if you like. I won't be offended, but I would like to challenge you.

I realize that most guys just want the "big picture," and that they don't like to get bogged down in the details. However, if you stick with reading the whole book, you may understand a little more about the princesses in your life. Remember the fairy godmother in the movie *Cinderella*, and how she helped Cinderella look so wonderful for the prince? Well, in real life it doesn't work that way. There is a far greater investment of time, effort and money involved. This is far more taxing on the modern princess, especially when it comes to preparing for an appearance with his royal highness. I'm sure the prince didn't ask what it took for Cinderella to look so great. And even if he had asked, he probably would have had a difficult time understanding all the fuss involved in the process. I can tell you this much, though: if Prince Charming had forgotten to compliment Cinderella that fateful night, the story would have had a very different ending. Just sayin'!

And fellas, it's not just about your girlfriend or your wife. It is about your teenage daughter who changes her hair every week as she tries to figure out her identity. It is about your sister who is trapped in a lonely marriage, or who is going through a painful divorce and just wants a new hairstyle to make her feel like a desirable woman again. It is about your mother, who wants her hair done every week, to make her feel respectable in social

9

settings, to make her feel like she's part of something bigger than herself (and possibly to impress those other women at Bridge Club on Thursday night). Hair matters to these women. And their hair roots begin in their hearts, pass through their minds, and are attached to their values.

*"If you change the way you look at things,
the things you look at change."*

Dr. Wayne Dyer

Hairy Godmother School

The Department of LLR (Labor, Licensing and Regulation) and the Board of Cosmetology protect the public by enforcing industry regulations that are required by each individual state. State agencies facilitate testing for fundamental professional service skills, and require that those with cosmetology licenses have an essential understanding of sterilization and sanitation. I fully support these components of our cosmetology licensing, as they are vital to public health and safety.

However, effective communication skills have been almost completely overlooked as a component of our cosmetology licensure. Operator techniques are taught in cosmetology schools with the understanding that the gift of time and practice will enhance those skills, but that isn't always enough.

The stylists who are fortunate enough to attend great schools or academies will develop business-building skills, customer service values, and learn branded signature techniques.

These academies include, but are not limited to Paul Mitchell, Redken, and Aveda, just to name a few. I would like to thank John Paul Mitchell Systems for the amazing education I received as one of their National Educators and Certified Color Educators. These certifications marked a huge turning point in my career, and I will be eternally grateful.

Many hairstylists are focused on enhancing their hairstyling and business skills in order to build, or maintain a loyal clientele. We love new products and, new ideas, and easily share our thoughts on them. Many stylists say that they are not salespeople, and that they don't like to push products. However, enthusiasm is contagious, as it creates a common connection and buzz for sales. This is a wonderful business asset for salons and stylists across the board.

I believe the most overlooked area in the salon industry, or in any other business for that matter, is the client consultation. Consultations are encouraged in the salon environment, but are commonly ineffective. Training with systemized and thorough communication techniques are desperately lacking in our industry.

More emphasis is needed on training in salon communications which will help prevent many disappointments in the salon environment. This will empower both the client and the stylist in the pursuit of desired and consistent results. Specific dialogue templates for effective consultation communications are indeed a rare find. It has been my experience that this specific training is almost nonexistent in the salon industry, especially when you consider the number of people who would benefit from this information.

Consultations can often go awry without this guidance, which causes unnecessary distress on both sides of the salon chair. Stylists often deal with conversations that are tense, or unpredictable in length, and so when feeling frustrated, they decide that there is no alternative but to shortcut the process. The problem is that too many people are just not feeling heard.

At best, consultations occur frequently, but effective communication does not. Discouragement generally leads to disconnection, or to accepting the status-quo, which is often veiled in cynicism.

Limited Powers

Just as we have an idea of our real-life Prince Charming and Cinderella, we have a general understanding that the ideal image is different for every person; and this is also true of our perception, especially when it comes to "real beauty," or what people say "looks good."

Hairy Godmothers can read minds and predict the future, right? I wish!

Let's think about this for a minute. How can our Hairy Godmother possibly grant wishes, especially if the only wishes she hears are confusing, and muddled with terminology that no one understands? We need communication guidelines, complete with a common dialogue that both clients and hairdressers understand.

Imagine if the fairy godmother in *Cinderella* was hard of hearing, and Cinderella felt certain that every word had been heard and was understood to bring her exactly what she needed. Would it have made a difference to Cinderella if the fairy godmother had used a *house* instead of *mouse* in her spell? It's only one letter, right? But the difference is drastic, which means the outcome is too.

This may seem like an extreme example, but it illustrates just how easily the little things can affect the desired end result.

Most words spoken in a salon setting are related to feeling, and so an emotional understanding is essential. The mechanics of cutting hair are learned in school, while the emotions of cutting hair can take years to master. We witness the emotional aspect of cutting hair on a daily basis, only without any real tangible guidance.

Clients are often just as bewildered as we are in terms of what to say. It's often difficult for them to articulate their ideas while understanding their options at the same time. When the goal is vague, the results will inevitably be unpredictable.

Most stylists are in the business because they love making people happy. When clients are unhappy, so are most stylists.

Even if it seems like no one cares, more often than not, they do. Many stylists have drowned in pools of negativity that they've encountered in their careers.

Others have found ways to protect their vulnerability by pretending that they "really don't care anymore," and by seeking a new path, keep their eyes glued to the nearest exit. I've known many stylists who struggled through the first few years of their career, sorely lacking in experience and guidance, and who paid a heavy emotional price. Emotions are deeply embedded in the perceived "magic" of the salon chair. Feelings are what move us and inspire us to thrive.

When a princess looks at her reflection with delight, it ignites the passion and creativity of her Hairy Godmother. Both are lifted by the experience of pure positivity.

Mirrored images can be transformed with combs, scissors and magical gels, but trust and connection are the real foundation of this magic.

Are you ready to discover your part in these most intimate ties and bring new magic to our salon experiences? Now, let's explore how we get in and out of salon relationship predicaments and bring a new awareness with a common language and solution we can all feel good about. Come with me and let's wave the wand together...

Chapter 2

Who is Your Hairy Godmother?

Your Hairy Godmother is your vision of the perfect hairstylist as *you* perceive it. She is unique to each of us, and understands our individual priorities. Yet, there is a common theme in who we are looking for, just as there is in that special someone in our romantic lives.

The fundamental qualities we look for in people are similar in both personal and professional relationships. To begin with, we generally want someone who is kind, considerate and who cares enough to listen. These characteristics are especially important in a professional service.

In addition, a person who is willing to go the extra mile in a business relationship sends a reassuring message to the client, reinforcing their commitment to customer service. This also enhances the culture of the business. Stylists who take the time to listen and appreciate their clients are living proof that Hairy Godmothers really do exist.

The road is very long and winding for the weary ones who trek in and out salons, searching for the right stylist. I have talked to a countless number of people, who have been searching for years. Most of them have lost hope that they will ever find a Hairy Godmother who will listen to them, and understand what they need while in the salon chair.

On more occasions than I can count, I've heard clients say, "There just aren't many good hair stylists out there." This has often been spoken in reference to personal relationships too. Many claim that dating is difficult, and that finding the perfect prince or princess is an arduous process.

Could these problems be connected? After all, the common denominator is *people*, in both personal and business relationships. Have we looked within ourselves to understand how we interact with others? What messages are we sending? Do we have realistic expectations of our stylists? Are we simply asking for too much?

People in successful relationships, both in business and personal relationships, enjoy the success of working as a team. Have you ever considered how empowering it would be to successfully collaborate new ideas while in the salon chair? How wonderful would it be to find a true professional who can be trusted to guide you through your decision? Does this sound like something you would want from a Hairy Godmother? Moreover, who *is* your Hairy Godmother? Let's explore more in this chapter and determine who it is you would like to meet in the salon castle.

I must address those who have been lucky enough to find their own true Hairy Godmother. If you have experienced the real magic in the salon castle with your very own Hairy Godmother, I imagine that you shudder at the thought of losing her. The idea of starting another long search, and sitting in unfamiliar salon chairs, can be overwhelming. Fear not! I have some ideas to help ease your concerns—especially if the unthinkable should happen, and you lose your Hairy Godmother.

Things are always changing in our lives. Often, circumstances appear to change out of nowhere. Sudden moves, illness, and death, for example, are all shocks to the system.

Losing a beloved hairstylist can be a traumatic experience. Over the years, I have met grieving clients who have lost their hairstylist due to tragic circumstances, such as death or terminal illness. It deeply affects clients, as the loss is similar to that of losing a family member or dear friend. Clients have shed their tears with me and I have been touched by their heartfelt loss. A new bond often develops through the grieving process— as an acknowledgement of the sadness begins the healing process. Bonds can easily form when losses have occurred on both sides of the chair.

Although losing a hairstylist can be very traumatic, I've found that leaving your beloved clients—from the stylist's end—is equally heart-wrenching. I was a hairstylist in the same town for sixteen years. I had no intention of leaving when I did, but one day I got a phone call that changed my life. My mother was diagnosed with a terminal brain tumor, and so I moved to a new town four hours away.

My clients and I were all in complete shock, as I relocated within two weeks of receiving the news. For almost eighteen months I would drive up on weekends and work with those who were willing to adapt to the uncertainty of my schedule. After my mother passed away, things became more complicated, as another relative of mine was diagnosed with cancer too. Eventually, I eventually had to make the painful decision to let go of those beloved clients that were left behind in my old town. It was devastating. It took a long time for me to recover, and I learned that many of my clients were having a hard time adjusting as well.

It's been almost twelve years now, and the good news is that I am still in touch with many of my former clients. Some of them have even visited me at my new salon. And as for those with whom I've lost touch, I hope they'll come across this book so they can understand how much they mean to me.

Recognizing Your Hairy Godmother

The bond between a hairstylist and her clients can take years to develop. This makes it harder initially to discern which hairstylist is the right fit for the person seated in the salon chair. Identifying and pursuing your perfect Hairy Godmother can be as challenging as finding a mate. Either way, it can be a bit hairy!

Generally, we find that women prioritize securing the perfect stylist to a greater degree than their male counterparts. For the most part, men don't have as many decisions to make when it comes to hair, fashion and makeup.

However, both men and women will benefit if they have an idea of what they are looking for before they venture out on a first date with anyone, and especially in the process of selecting a Hairy Godmother. If you don't know what you want in a person, you are most likely to end up with someone you *don't* want. The same principle applies to finding your Hairy Godmother

What's Important to You?

What do you look for in a stylist? Generally, we consider factors like time, money and value of experience. I find that initially people are invested in the end result more than they are in their stylist. After all, it's just hair, right? Hmmm, I'll let you be the judge of that.

My experience has taught me that it becomes more of a priority to focus on finding a good stylist after a disappointing experience has occurred in a salon. This sense of frustration motivates clients to look in another place, but unfortunately by then, the new priority is a focus on correcting a problem rather than reaching an optimum goal.

The optimal goal is to connect with a stylist who offers consistent performance, and who can meet the client's needs with a great service value. Ideally, this should be in an environment that is both comfortable and enjoyable. Availability and convenience are important, but not always essential for those searching for the right stylist. Clients will travel many miles, especially if the salon experience is an important enough priority to feel safe in a salon chair.

What Does Your Ideal Appointment Look Like to You?

When a client enters our salon, she is greeted with a warm smile and confident handshake before she is escorted to a seat in the reception area. Once she's been offered a beverage, we hand her a small clipboard and a pen so she can complete a client data card. (We don't offer alcoholic beverages in our salon…bad spells could arise from that!)

Take a look at the sample form and ask yourself the following questions, rating them from 1 to 5. It's not a survey; rather, the purpose of this form is to identify what's important to you in a visit to the salon. Take your time as you consider each answer. Filling out a form can be a hassle, but I promise you that this is a sure way to avoid an even bigger hassle in the salon chair.

Most people already know whether their priority is a reasonably priced salon, with a convenient location and a short wait time, over a more a specialized experience. However, they may not be aware of *why* something is important until they think about it.

Knowing why we make the choices we do opens up the possibility for even better options. We often get locked in our habits and assumptions, which limits other opportunities offering more benefit. Often, we choose what's right in front of us simply because it's *there*, and so we risk forfeiting the options we didn't even know we had. The first step in finding what you want is being clear enough to recognize it.

Client Service Priority Form

	Not So Important	Somewhat Important	Important	Very Important	Essential
Convenience	①	②	③	④	⑤
Cost	①	②	③	④	⑤
Overall Experience	①	②	③	④	⑤
Salon Environment	①	②	③	④	⑤
Choice of Stylist	①	②	③	④	⑤
Color Specialist	①	②	③	④	⑤
Hair Cut Specialist	①	②	③	④	⑤
Shampoo Massage	①	②	③	④	⑤
Blowout & Style	①	②	③	④	⑤
Consultation Communication	①	②	③	④	⑤

Additional remarks or specifications

This form is where clients can give us some insight into their story. We want to know what they want, what they want to avoid, and what we can do to exceed their expectations each and every time. In addition, this form reveals our intent to listen and discover what is important to all our princes and princesses. There is a section for the client to write a quick note or remark, and we ask the client to write the most important thing he or she wants us to know about their hair, or their ideal hair salon experience. We explain that we will be keeping these notes in their client file, which we will store in our computer system to maintain efficient accuracy. We inform the client that our goal is to develop consistency through identifying what is important to her each and every visit.

We also do this for our out-of-town guests. We find that they often schedule appointments each time they are in town, and so we maintain a record of their experience and service priorities. When we ask them why they keep coming back to our salon, the answer is generally the same: because we were friendly and they felt like we listened to them.

Answering these questions can be hard, especially without having much time to contemplate each response. I invite clients to review their answers at the end of their hair appointment, and we'll help them clarify what's important to them. We are told over and over again that no one has ever asked them these kinds of questions before. Has anyone ever asked you what you prioritize in a salon? How about when you've visited other service industry businesses? Imagine for a moment what that would be like. What would you say? How clear are you about what you want?

Oftentimes, clients look stunned, and even panicked, when asked questions as specific as ours. They may need a little coaching, with suggestions such as "Don't cut my bangs to short," or "Cowlick in the crown," or "Please don't make my hair too dark." We've even heard, "I want to leave with both ears intact!"

Imagine walking into a restaurant, and while you were waiting for your drinks, the waiter asks, "Could you please write down what we can do to make this the best dining experience you've ever had?" Most service industries ask for feedback *after* the service. The problem is, *after the service,* it is too late to ask the client what they want. Suppose your waiter read your suggestions before you arrived at the establishment and said, "I see that you want your drinks refilled quietly so that you can talk and not be disturbed. You would like your food hot and paced appropriately for the ultimate dining experience, and that you would like it very much if I brought you the check without you having to ask or hunt me down."

Can you imagine the kitchen and wait staff delivering exactly what you asked for? At our salon, we aim to accommodate every client's needs, which is why we ask these questions before we pick up a pair of scissors or color brush.

This method helps us avoid making mistakes, so that we can focus on our clients' desired outcomes, and most importantly, so that our clients feel heard. However, I have learned that some clients are intimidated by the daunting task of articulating their requests. They may feel uncomfortable about asking for specific things, even if they know exactly what they want. Clients may feel like they are being put on the spot, and they'd rather keep their thoughts to themselves than risk being seen as demanding, unrealistic or unqualified to make suggestions.

A simple information form, not unlike the one in this chapter, can offer a platform to express vital information from the first visit, which will set the tone for the entire professional relationship. Once you have completed your Client Priority Form, you may be able to identify the type of Hairy Godmother that works best for you.

To some, it may seem as though the main goal is just a good cut or color, but generally we go to a salon because we want to feel good, either while we're there or after the service has been completed—or both. Regardless, we go to the salon because we want to feel better. However, the emotional influence of hair and salon experience is not obvious to everyone in the ways you would imagine. Whether we stick with the same stylist often depends on our personalities, and what's going on in our lives.

When we choose a hairstylist, we look for someone who can give us an emotional benefit that begins at the salon, with continued emotional benefits outside the salon, whether we're aware of these benefits or not.

Here is a general list of the different types of stylists you may encounter. I have listed the emotional benefits of each one. Take a look at the list and see if you can identify *your* stylist, and the emotion you associate with your Hairy Godmother.

Examples of Hairy Godmother Attributes and Emotional Benefits

1. **Collaborative Stylist**: Shares ideas and thoughts with you. You are a team.

   Emotional Benefit: It's about feeling heard and being a part of the process.

2. **Polite Stylist:** Always pleasant, never disagrees...doesn't bother you with unwarranted alternative ideas.

   Emotional Benefit: Safe, easy, conflict-free.

3. **Consistent Stylist:** Doesn't like changing things. Stays inside the box; reliable and motivated by routine.

   Emotional Benefit: Safe, free of risks.

4. **Entertaining Stylist**: Always fun and exciting to see this personality, although the hair matters, it's not just about the hair. It's more about the connection and the experience.

   Emotional Benefit: Uplifting, comfortable, makes for a fun escape.

5. **Counselor Stylist:** Shows interest in your life. The salon experience is more about friendship and trust than the hair.

   Emotional Benefit: Safe, fulfilling. Enhances one's sense of belonging and loyalty.

6. **Young, Hip Stylist**: It's about the hair, and a perception of youth. New and fresh ideas. Keeps tabs on current trends.

   Emotional Benefit: Excitement and empowerment in feeling young with freedom of expression in creativity.

7. **Older, Experienced Stylist**: Takes control of situation when needed. Margin for error is minimized due to experience.

   Emotional Benefit: Trust and certainty. Safety, security.

8. **Business-Only Stylist**: Gets you in, only to get you out as soon as possible. No fuss. No discussion. It's all about efficiency.

   Emotional Benefit: Emotional freedom, easy access without obligation. Convenience.

9. **Creative Genius Stylist**: It's about the
   possibilities and the potential to stand out in
   a crowd. Focused on how you'll feel when
   you leave.

   Emotional Benefit: Freedom, and emphasis
   on the value of individual expression;
   fearless and carefree.

Misunderstood Hairy Godmothers

In defense of hairstylists who haven't asked their
clients the questions mentioned in this chapter, I must
say that it's not that they don't care. Rather, it's that
there hasn't been a whole lot of focus on coaching and
communication with clients in our industry as a whole.
We have been encouraged to give consultations, but
our main focus is on giving clients what they want
and developing the skills to deliver it to the best of our
abilities. This is very different from understanding the
perception of what the client is asking for.

I, for one, believe it is my job to help people understand
their perceptions and manage their expectations. Then,
as a professional, I must help them clarify their priorities
to guide them through the best options available to
them. Through this process, they feel more empowered
to make informed decisions, and will consider all their
options before making a decision.

Clients have experienced horrific results from
misunderstanding what they were asking for. As the
old saying goes- *Be careful what you wish for because
you just might get it.* This is why you need a Hairy

Godmother who you can talk to, and who will really listen with her ears, her eyes, and her heart!

Whose Chair Are You Sitting In?

Speaking of Hairy Godmother's and hairstylists, whose chair are you sitting in at the salon?

And more importantly, how do you feel about it?

If you are in a complicated hairdresser relationship, don't worry—the following chapters will help you clear the mist. It is my goal to help you find solutions through empowerment, and to help you identify how to set and reset boundaries. I encourage you to keep reading this book. If it is time to make a change, and you don't know when and how to do so, we will delve deeper into what you really want. We'll walk you through your decision, and help you see things more clearly the next time around.

The goal is to find your real Hairy Godmother, the one who will ultimately protect you from a run-in with the ugly stepsisters, Lady Doubt and Lady Fear; and let's not forget the evil stepmother, the Countess of Shame. This family of negative emotions can influence so many of our decisions. You and Your Hairy Godmother, however, will work as a team to discover and strengthen the positive things you see in your reflection.

The Prince, the Princess and Her Hairy Godmother

I mentioned how looking for the right hairdresser is similar to finding a mate, as both are arduous processes. I think this story illustrates the connection between true love and a person's Hairy Godmother, and so I thought I would share it with you.

Staci and I met in 2010. She was referred to me by James, the man she would later marry. James was a financial officer at the auto dealership where I bought a car for my daughter. As he scanned over my forms, he quickly noticed that I was a hairdresser and began to ask me about where I worked. His face lit up as he pulled out a picture of a beautiful blonde lady and began to tell me about the girl he going to marry. He wanted to set up an appointment for Staci, his anticipated bride to be. The proposal was imminent, set to take place at a surprise weekend getaway at the Biltmore Estates in North Carolina. James explained that his fiancé was trapped in a bad hairdresser relationship, and Staci's golden locks were at great risk (as well as his growing concern for her, as she continuously left the salon in a state of distress). Staci lived two hours away at the time, on the other side of Charleston, South Carolina, but James assured me that she would want to make the drive to try her hand at a new hairstylist. I found the situation unrealistic at first, doubting that Staci would drive two hours for an appointment with me, but James was adamant. I guess it may have been because James had run my credit report, and so he knew I wasn't shady. As he started to tell more about Staci's demise, I think he could read the compassion in my face. I connected

29

with him, and admired the way he cared for his girl. He knew I cared about her situation, and I knew that he connected to that as well.

He was so ardent about her wellbeing that I knew he was reaching out to me for help. How could I not help this Prince Charming? So, needless to say, the car contract was not the only promise I made that day.

True to his word, James convinced Staci to reach out to me a few days later. After seating her in my salon chair, I found that not only was she absolutely gorgeous, with a dazzling white smile, shimmering brown eyes and a beach-tan glow, but Staci was an absolute sweetheart. As she looked at her reflection, she expressed sadness and disgust, noticing only the broken hair framing her face, with her shoulder length hair resting around her neck. The ends were frayed from repeated over processed bleach applications.

Of course, I secretly knew that Prince Charming was going to propose to this beautiful princess, and so I knew how important it was that she feel very special and beautiful. I talked to her and discovered that her *biggest priority* was growing her hair out longer again. She didn't want it to be at shoulder length. Moreover, she was frustrated with her previous stylist as she had to keep getting her hair "trimmed" or "cut" in order to manage the ends. Previously, her hair seemed to get shorter and shorter, and frizzier each time she visited her local salon. During her first appointment with me I promised that I wouldn't cut it, despite the fact it desperately needed a trim. Instead, I decided to focus on repair treatments. We agreed to bring down the color a little some with lowlights. I showed Staci some options for her hair so that she could give up her high-temperature flat iron. I explained that it would take several months to see a dramatic difference in the condition and length of her hair, but I assured her that she would notice changes soon enough. In addition, I explained that we would need to trim her hair just a bit to keep it from fraying even more on the next visit. I suggested fractional dusting of the ends with small frequent visits at first, until the irreversible damage was gone. Staci understood that I wanted to help her and that I respected her wishes. She needed to feel heard, and so we were able to work together for a solution. She left happy and feeling much better, and returned to her next appointment with a ring on her finger, looking even more radiant and beautiful than ever. James and Staci married the following year, and since then have become loyal clients.

They had been married for a couple of years when James called me, in need of an urgent haircut. This was not uncommon for him, as he had a hectic schedule at the car dealership, which was over twenty miles away. However, it was Christmastime, and even though I had accommodated him many times before—he would come in early or late, with little or no notice—I just simply couldn't do it that day. Staci had been scheduled for that same day for weeks, but James wanted me to work him in, with her, while she was processing. Her processing time was tricky, and often shorter than his allotted haircut time, and I was unwilling to jeopardize Staci's hair—not even for her husband! James, needless to say, was not happy and he gave my receptionist a very hard time. He immediately called Staci to complain about me, and it was then that he was taken by surprise:

Staci was furious with him, and she let him have it! I still can't believe it, but Staci brought that bad prince into the salon and made him apologize to us.

She said, "I told him I can find another man, but a good hairdresser is too hard to find!" He came in after he realized what was at stake for him. Hell hath no fury like a woman scorned! I was not upset with James. I've been around long enough to know that this man is a good man.

James is one of the toughest men I know. He is super smart, and understands that behind every happily married man is a happy wife. James politely called back the next day for an appointment. Our staff greeted him with his favorite coffee cake and morning soda, served on a personal tray. We rewarded him for good behavior—it's been over five years now, and I adore both Staci and James. In fact, I consider them true friends.

So, what did we learn here? James really loves Staci. And Staci really loves James. Nobody is perfect, and that doesn't mean we're bad people. But the real lesson in this story is…let no man or prince come between the princess and her Hairy Godmother, even if he was the one who found her!

Chapter 3

Who's Looking in the Magic Mirror?

In the story of Snow White, the queen asks the magic mirror to tell her who the fairest in the land is, and the mirror's response is "Snow White". The queen becomes enraged when she learns of this. This news ignites a burning desire to snuff out Snow White. The truth is, the queen is obsessed, longing for the assurance that *she* is the most beautiful in the land.

It's worth noting here that it wasn't Snow White's *physical beauty* that made her the "fairest" in the land —It was her gentle grace. More often than not, when people read the story or watch movies related to it, the focus has been on Snow White's physical beauty.

The queen was so consumed with the possibility of Snow White being a threat; she did extreme things to achieve her elusive goal of being the fairest one of all.

Ironically, she was willing to take on the form of an old beggar woman, warts and all, in order to achieve this. She became warped in her thinking, forgetting that she was already a famed beauty in her own right.

Can you think of a beautiful famous person who has felt pressured to retain their movie star image? Do you know of anyone who has succumbed to these societal and industry pressures? There are many who are willing to go under the knife repeatedly or do whatever else is necessary. The pressure can be excessive.

Do you know of a beautiful person who has been so obsessed with how they look, never realizing their own beauty, and focusing only on the flaws that ultimately strip away their confidence? I've seen this distorted sense of self many times in the salon.

Society plays a huge role in our self-perception. Social opinions and expectations influence how we look at ourselves, and essentially dictate what we should project into the social arena.

Since the dawn of fashion, our personal images and esteems have been tossed about in the trends of what is deemed beautiful and acceptable. Attachment to outside opinions only seems to complicate our inner world.

The way we see our reflection can often be influenced by others. It often supersedes who we are as a "whole person," and our inner truth. These programmed ideas alter our perception and subsequently affect how we interact with others.

I have witnessed countless times, the most unkind inner-critics, those who express nothing more than negative self-talk while seated in front the salon mirror, no matter how beautiful they are. I hear them comment on round faces, big ears, big nose, squinty or baggy eyes, sagging skin or ugly necks; and I often hear mention of their need for potential plastic surgeries, or at the very least a general focus on every potential flaw.

Oftentimes, these are things that no one else would ever notice. It is amazing how our minds can distort our vision and create imperfections that, to others, simply do not exist. It is truly heartbreaking to see people pull themselves apart; and what's worse, they are so used to thinking in that way, that they are not even aware they're doing it. I've even been guilty of it myself.

Few have escaped the snares of negative self-talk. I feel that we all have succumbed to it at some point in our lives. It is tied to the journey of building self-confidence, through the perceptions of measured successes, and also with the scars of defeat and trauma that we've suffered along the way. The deepest roots lie in the way we compare ourselves to others, which often confuses our self-worth.

As a stylist, I've noticed that men seem less openly vulnerable in front of the salon mirror. They are generally much more stoic in my chair, especially in their first few appointments. Men's self- assessments seem to be more private, preferring to keep their negative self-talk within the confines of their own bathrooms. They may only share their body image issues with their wives and girlfriends.

I have to admit that I've laughed with the ladies over the years as they've shared eyewitness accounts of bathroom mirror scenes with their husbands. I've heard of stories taking place in master bathrooms, of men posing with flexed muscles, admiring themselves with masculine expressions of approval.

Traditionally, men have been programmed to be tough, and so tend to be more poker faced than women, especially when it comes to public displays of vulnerability. However, confidence levels and self-esteem are considered gender neutral. We all need to feel good about ourselves, and it's healthier when it starts from the inside, moving outward.

It is important to understand how strongly these perceptions are attached to a person's needs, wants and desires and to the way we move through life. Even though we all have images we'd like to maintain, our inner beings are shaped by the passions we are drawn to, and are unique to each of us. Personal style and individual expression can be as distinctive as our physical features. This is particularly important to grasp while in the salon, as it affects the expectations of the client, as well as the stylist's perceived ability to deliver those expectations. The most important task of even the greatest and most talented stylists, is to master the understanding of the client's perceptions and expectations.

Ken's Tale

Ken is a master stylist and instructor. He is an amazing artist, and admired by many in the field, as Ken understands every aspect of cutting and coloring hair. One day, we were sharing some of our experiences with clients, and Ken told me of a valuable lesson he learned from a client he had worked with years ago, in his upscale salon in New Jersey.

It was over twenty-five years ago when a beautiful African American woman walked into his salon. "She was stunning!" Ken remarked. She was sweet, quiet-natured and seemed open to anything he said. She'd heard he was the best, and had complete faith in him. Consequently, she had no issue with the salon chair being turned away from the mirror while Ken worked on her hair.

After a few hours in the salon Ken transformed this beauty by bestowing a classic asymmetrical sculpted style on her head. He called it the *Raspberry Beret*. This work of art was tilted and perfectly angled to accent her delicate features. His eyes were still lighting up as he recalled his work of art and the glorious raspberry red color he'd specially formulated.

He was so excited for the beautiful lady, who seemed pleased with the end result. She did mention that it might take her husband some getting used to, but Ken reassured her of how gorgeous she looked as he escorted her to the reception counter for check out.

Other people in the salon offered encouraging remarks of their own, marveling at the avant-garde style. It wasn't until she wrote her check for this amazing salon service that Ken saw her name, and realized that she was the wife of a church minister. He was horrified that he had created this beautiful modern masterpiece, for this particular woman, as the style would have been more appropriate in a New York City night club than a Sunday morning church service. Fortunately for Ken, the lady was mild-mannered, and was willing to bravely face her potential critics. She returned less than a week later to soften the look and make it a little less dramatic.

It doesn't matter how capable stylists are, it is crucial to pay attention to more than just the hair. Our individual styles are expressed in the choices we make in hair, makeup and dress. It's not only the style of clothes, but it's how they fit as well. Our choice to wear makeup is as significant as the way in which we wear it. Jewelry, purses and shoes all express our tastes and the way we feel about ourselves, and our relationship with society.

As a hairdresser, I strive to put these things in to a clear and balanced perspective by considering all the information available. I really like to take my time getting to know the client in every consultation. Oftentimes, I can see clients approaching through the salon window and catch a glimpse of them walking across the parking lot toward the salon; and my work begins at that very moment. Body language, posture and style of dress offer clues about a person's personality and individual style.

Body Language

Upon the client's arrival, I observe their body language, as this helps me identify signs of restlessness, tension or sometimes ease. As we become more digitalized, and move in to a more virtual world with our younger generations, it seems that organic conversations in the waiting area of a salon have become much less common than they were in the past. Many prefer retreating to the virtual world of their smartphones. It seems that we are not in the habit of fully engaging with one another in face-to-face conversations. Not like we did in the previous decades, before mobile devices.

In essence, the way we interact with one another has changed. Body language is timeless and transcends the evolution of verbal communication. The way clients enter and exit the salon give clues regarding the success of the visit. I pay attention to facial expressions, particularly in the eyes and brow area. Quick, jerky body movements imply tension and nervousness, or worse, dissatisfaction.

On the other hand, a slow pace with more controlled movements indicates a more laid-back personality. A bubbly, outgoing person smiles a lot, makes eye contact and appears eager to engage. So many little vibes can set the tone for the entire appointment's interaction.

The waiting area is a great place to get a bearing on clients' needs. Prior to the haircut, while they are waiting, clients often play with the part of their hair that bothers them the most. Consequently, I casually observe how they play with their hair and identify some of their concerns non-verbally. Shorter-haired clients will fiddle with their bangs, or with the heaviness in certain areas at the back of the head and crown. Long-haired clients often sit, stretching their hair in a downward motion. I see them gathering it into long, side-swept ponytails, stretching their hair with bent necks and lowered chins in order to create a closer vantage point for their self-evaluation. They take inventory of their split ends, contemplating how much length will have to be sacrificed. And I bet you thought no one noticed you!

Many clients will sift frantically through hair magazines, or sit staring at a montage of smart phone images they have collected in their various online accounts, as they wrestle with self-doubt or battle with confusion. Few sit staring at these images with the confidence that their vision is about to be fulfilled, but yet will still remain hopeful.

Style of Dress

When clients sit in the reception area, I notice the way they wear their makeup, or if they don't wear any at all. Minimal makeup often leads to very natural hairstyles. These clients prefer not to use much product in their hair. A client's attention to detail in the application of their makeup shows me that they are very style savvy. Their view of makeup shows me whether a client is willing to invest time in her appearance. If the application is heavy or intricate, then I sense that style is important to her, and that she probably prioritizes the look and color of her haircut, as opposed to easy carefree wash and wear with no maintenance. This client is usually not opposed to picking up a blow dryer, curling iron or flat iron, and is open to use styling products. Furthermore, she is likely to invest a reasonable amount of time (meaning somewhere around thirty to forty-five minutes) in her daily routine to achieve her look.

Clients' style of dress, even if they have just come from the gym, gives me clues too. Activewear is a trend in and of itself these days!

Conversely, loose clothes don't necessarily imply that a person is sloppy and that they don't want to draw attention to their shape or size. It might be a style preference, or just a desire for comfort. When they're paired with trendy jewelry, loose clothing can look very chic. And it goes without saying how much shoes influence our style. These are all very important indicators for a stylist to consider when selecting options for their client.

Shoes and purses give clues for a client's preference in hair choices. The style, brand, color, as well as the size and the way they are carried are clues to a personality. Shoes are in a league all of their own; I especially observe the way clients walk, as this often helps to indicate their level of ease and confidence.

There is a lot more to cutting hair than just snipping off dead ends. It is my job to discover and identify the client's primary goal. I assess the investment of her time, effort and budget, and take all that into account when I cultivate her desired look. I also consider and explain maintenance issues, and how to preserve the condition of the hair, especially in the long term. I need to offer alternative solutions to unreasonable requests. I must develop the best plan, and align it with a reality that she can live with, and hopefully embrace. I have to relay any maintenance pitfalls for chemical services, and help her decide on the best option available. This can get tricky, as I have to find a way to be clear and direct without offending her—I've learned that one the hard way. There is no greater teacher than experience, and the more painful the experience, the more you learn.

I have talked a lot about the complexities of who is looking into the magic mirror, but not everyone is that complicated. There are many, many, clients who hold priorities that they themselves would consider greater than their reflected mirror image. I often hear the statement, "Just do whatever you think will look nice." I have to identify what "nice" means, though. Make no mistake that the hair is still important, but many clients don't want to spend a whole lot of time on their hair each day. We have to be very careful in these cases, as vague requests tend to bring about vague results. It is important to target the priority, even if the request appears simple.

In the last chapter, we looked over some general characteristics of hairstylists and their performance styles. Clients have some characteristics that can give a hairdresser the heads up on how to handle an incoming client on any given day. Client and stylists can affect each other during interactions with non-verbal communication. Ultimately, the main objective of a hairdresser is to be attentive, and to recognize the consistencies in the client's requests and behaviors. We know when something is wrong with our friends and our loved ones, and even with our pets for that matter. Sometimes someone is just having a bad day, and unless you are really familiar with a person, you may not see that. It can happen on both sides of the chair. We often fail to realize what other people are going through.

The Quiet Princess

Sue has always been a sweet, low-maintenance lady. She is loyal, kind and often very quiet. She doesn't talk a whole lot and doesn't spend much time gazing at herself in the mirror. Her first appointment with me was about ten years ago when she walked in and asked for a simple haircut. I suggested a "spotlight," which is a special highlight feature, trendy at the time, and I offered it "on the house," and Sue accepted. I was new to the area and wanted to build a strong clientele of great people like Sue.

She had never considered color before, and had always steered clear of high-maintenance styles, but she loved the splash of gold in her bang area. And this style met her criteria, as it required minimal efforts to maintain; and plus, now she had a fun new look. She returned to me every other month, and over time our connection grew. She even worked around my schedule during a rough time in my life, when my son was in a terrifying car accident and I took time off work. I grew more and more fond of her as she revealed her quiet compassion for me.

A few years ago Sue, the Quiet Princess, came into the salon in her usual way. She sat in the waiting area and smiled her sweet smile. I finished up the client I was working on and invited Sue to sit in the styling chair. We had the usual check in consultation, and then I ushered Sue back to the shampoo bowl. I took a look at her and asked how she was doing and knew that something wasn't right in the way she answered, "Okay, but not great," She smiled a half-smile. It was so subtle that if I hadn't known her, I may have missed it completely.

I paused for a few seconds and looked directly at her. Sue shrugged her shoulders, as we made eye contact, thinking she had escaped my concern. I gently nudged her to elaborate on what was going on; and she disclosed quietly to me that her mother had suddenly passed, and that her husband had been diagnosed with prostate cancer. It was close to the holidays, and she mentioned, almost casually that she would be glad for the year to be over, as it had "...not been the best year."

I was stunned by the news and marveled at how calm she was. She probably hadn't discussed it with too many people, even though Sue is a pharmacist and beloved by many in the community. She is not the type to complain. As they say, still waters run deep.

The appointment went on as normal, but I was affected by Sue's struggles. I wanted to do more, but I could only offer Sue a private text later that day, and share a quiet understanding with Sue of how much I cared.

There have been others who have come in, and I could sense immediately that things were not right. These lovely princesses, whom I have come to know and love would sometimes reveal a restlessness, or uneasiness in front of the mirror that seemed out of character for them.

The advantage of having a hairstylist that you feel connected to is a true blessing for both the stylist and the client she serves. If you have ever experienced this magic, you know that there is nothing like it. Your Hairy Godmother is a person that truly wants the best for you.

She will do everything in her power to help you see the real beauty that lives in your reflection when you look in to the magic mirror, even when you aren't feeling your best.

Chapter 4

Your Hairy Godmother is Out There!

We've explored what you need from your Hairy Godmother, so now it's time to get out there and find her. It's smart to have a strategy as you conduct a mindful search for your perfect match. There are various ways that you can get a good referral.

When you spot a good color and well-shaped cut, this can be a beacon to guide you to the right place. It is important to decide how far are you willing to travel to get your hair done. How frequently will you need to visit the salon? These are just a few factors to consider as you search for your Hairy Godmother. I have clients who drive lengthy distances, and some that even return year after year from outside of the country. I am touched by their loyalty, yet I am willing to share custody with other hairdressers in order to offer them the best service.

This next story illustrates things to consider in deciding how far is too far, so I thought I would share it with you…

Andrea's Tale

Andrea told me her tale the very first day she came into our salon. She was looking for a new salon home base after having gone to the same stylist for many years; she thought her former stylist was really great, but unfortunately had moved away. Andrea looked forward to those monthly appointments with her stylist and enjoyed being in the salon chair. Andrea said that even though her beloved stylist had moved only forty-five miles away, she decided that the distance was simply too great, although she did explain that this was in no way a reflection of the affection she had for her stylist.

This wasn't the first time Andrea had gone through something like this. She had been in the same predicament when she lived just outside Atlanta, Georgia many years ago. At that time, she had opted to stay with her stylist and make the hour long trek to the city from her suburban home.

She knew that there would be a combined two hours of travel, and an additional two hours for the salon appointment. Andrea adjusted by making a day of her hair appointment, with shopping and dining, offsetting the inconvenience.

At first she looked forward to her monthly excursion to the city. Eventually, however, Andrea began to dread her hair appointments. It occurred to her that it had become much more of a hassle than it was worth, what with the traffic and the time involved. She realized that she wanted to look forward to her appointments, and that the long drive negated the benefits of sitting in the salon chair of her wonderful stylist. When her second stylist moved away, Andrea knew right away that she would simply have to start looking for another one, closer to home.

The First Steps of Your Journey

Here are some things to consider as you begin your search. I have categorized the sources and included an opinion based on the feedback and experiences that both my clients and I have personally experienced. As you read through the list, you may relate to some of them yourself, and hopefully you will learn something new. I'm certain, however, of the commonality of these situations. Remember that you're not alone in the quest for your Hairy Godmother!

A Cautionary Note:

> I find that my clients with naturally great hair are the ones who are most often asked the question, "Who does your hair?" In these cases, my work likely showcases an enhanced look on a preexisting beautiful crown of hair. Oftentimes, these compliments are bestowed upon ladies who spend time accentuating their look, with style and finish.

> The cut creates the shape, while the style creates the finished look. I am always pleased when I receive glowing reviews from new referrals, but in all honesty, I can't take the credit for naturally great hair that is stunning in any setting, any more than I can take blame for thin, fine hair that struggles to find its best look. It is wise to

47

consider hairstyles on ladies who appear to have similar hair textures to yours. If you see something you like, ask!

Grocery Stores

Standing in the checkout line at the grocery store, you'll be able to see plenty of great haircuts up-close, and from all angles. Not to mention, you can ask questions and get a real live review that may lead to a potential candidate for a new hairstylist.

You're getting this information firsthand, and so this is the most authentic kind of review you'll find. The advantage of a referral like this one is that it's practically anonymous! There is no expectation or pressure for you to follow the advice of these women in the checkout line, especially if you decide not to follow up on their recommendations.

You may decide to boycott the idea altogether because you discover the salon is in an inconvenient location, or perhaps you've simply found a better option. There's also a good chance that people in grocery stores are in everyday clothes with a true everyday look.

Happy clients often enjoy being walking advertisements for their beloved hairdressers. Maybe you feel awkward talking to someone about their hair at the grocery store—but don't! Who doesn't like to receive compliments? Especially when it's about having great hair. After all, you could make someone's day. As we learned in Sue's tale back in Chapter 3, you may never know who might benefit from a kind word.

It's also a good idea to have a pen handy in the checkout line so you can clarify the name and number of the referral. A simpler plan is to log the information directly into your smart phone and mark it in the *Contacts* section. For example, save the stylist's name as *Hair/ Michelle*. This way you are less likely forget the name of the stylist!

Online

There are all kinds of online referral services that offer resources and information on where to get a good haircut. You can look up local hair salons on Google or Yelp and see people's reviews—and it's a good idea to read as many reviews as you can on each salon. Don't let one bad review sway you too much, because not every match is a perfect one. Salons may encounter damaging remarks when there's just one bad stylist in a group of very good ones. Look for names in the reviews wherever possible; and if you see one name pop up, make a note of it.

If you see only one bad review after a string of good ones, and if the stylist's name is mentioned in that bad review, keep in mind that the stylist could have just had a bad day (it happens to all of us). The reviewer, on the other hand, may have had a skewed experience to report. Look for repetition rather than basing your opinion on just one review. Overall, there will be a dominant theme of positivity or negativity in all of them, and so I recommend reading several reviews, even as many as a dozen, for each salon.

In these instances, the majority opinion rules. Keep in mind a review is just an opinion, and an arrow pointing in one direction. Browse your favorite social media sites and see what other people may recommend. You will get all sorts of responses, and so be prepared to ask the right questions, and to filter through them all until you see some consistency.

Even after all of this, you may still come up empty-handed, even after reading reviews and visiting a salon—but these are definitely effective points of reference. Remember the priorities you have established for yourself. This will be your internal guide. Look for reviews that show more positive remarks in the specific areas of interest that are the most important to you.

Neighbors, Friends and Family

Neighbors, friends and family are wonderful people to have in your life. They care about you and your happiness. It's only natural that when we find something wonderful, we want to share it with the people we love. Right?

We feel a sense of duty to lead them to the Promised Land and share the good news. This is especially true if we know of someone whose hair needs work and we appoint ourselves to help them. How can we keep this wonderful secret when we have personally discovered the fountain of youth? In our eagerness to help, we may forget how our recommendations sound when our words are landing on someone else's ears, so be careful how you approach this.

In some circles, health and beauty have pretty much become a first-world religion. Friends and neighbors can be so passionate about these topics that we have to be careful not to push or reject advice that is intended to "help" us. A hairstylist recommendation from someone close to us can be wonderful and exciting, especially when friends of ours have seemingly found the answers to their hair struggles. I have had neighborhood groups and friendship circles that delight in surprise salon meetings, and who have even shared color processing times together. They truly enjoy their bonus time and fun experiences.

A word of caution, though—please keep in mind that if you ever fall into a rift with a friend, neighbor or relative who has referred you to her stylist, then you may not want to run in to her unexpectedly at the salon. Conversely, if you refer a friend and things don't go well at the salon, be advised that she will almost certainly come to you and share her experience. A good or bad experience can affect the relationship with your friend and neighbor, especially if you expect to stay with your beloved Hairy Godmother.

You may want to consider your friend's general attitude before you put yourself out there. If you feel that you wouldn't enjoy being at the salon with your friend for a couple of hours, then this will more than likely be hard on your Hairy Godmother too.

As much as you love your friend, neighbor or relative, you may find that you want to go to a stylist who isn't tied to your inner circle outside the salon. Having said this, my business has flourished on friends referring friends. For the most part, I have witnessed many friendships thrive both in and outside of the salon.

Spouse

Husbands and wives often go to different types of salons, as their hair preferences rarely overlap. Occasionally, women send in their re-con husbands. This is the undercover scout who is willing to partner with his queen on the quest to find the perfect stylist. He may work as a lone wolf or pair as a tag team with his lady. The tag team is very stealth, as the man is willing lay his hairline down for his queen, while she appears to casually flip through magazines, yet is covertly paying attention to every nuance in the salon. My theory is that, for him, there is usually less hair at risk than his long-haired queen, so he's willing to put his strands on the line and go undercover for the woman he loves. What a prince!

I have had couples confess this M.O. after our relationship has been established, and we have all enjoyed a laugh over it. Just so you know. re-con husbands ... we're on to you! And a word of advice ladies: don't send him in to get your products if you can help it. Once they know how much you spend, you may be at risk for extreme rationing.

Sometimes it's a wife who's had such a great experience in a salon that she'll recommend a stylist, or even schedule her husband an appointment, before she leaves. The husband may not share the same view, and after a visit or two, he may very well move on. His experience in the same salon might not meet his priorities in the same way as his wife. With no harm done, it is not uncommon for him to move on after a brief time with us. We are a small studio salon, and we understand completely that there are times when the king must return to his own castle. It's always a pleasure to meet my client's "other halves," and satisfy the curiosity of putting the face to the name. His queen will often stay on with us, for years enjoying her salon castle.

I've had couples who have been seeing me for years, and it is a wonderful privilege to spend times with the happily married ones. It inspires me to see how deep the bonds of friendship can be in a marriage as it is truly a beautiful thing to behold. I love looking at these people in the mirror. I learn so much from their humor and interactions. On the flip-side however, it can be difficult to navigate through appointments with couples who are no longer fond of each other.

They may have started out happily enough when they first joined forces in salon visits, but over time I could see the corrosion forming in their marriage. It's hard to watch and steer clear of the dangerous currents of these murky waters.

At times, I've felt more like a maid or valet on *Downton Abbey*, sharing guarded feedback each time I've been put on the spot. I even have the British accent! It is indeed a slippery slope. After all, who gets the hairdresser in the divorce agreement?

Clubs You Attend

Are you a member of a gym, golf, bridge or tennis club, or any club at all? Well, organizations can be great sources for referrals, especially when it comes to finding a good hair stylist who will meet your needs. If you see a hairstyle that you like and it appears to be suited to your daily life, then you may want to ask for a referral. As I pointed out earlier in the chapter, there is a risk of a possible "too close for comfort" situation at the salon, but usually you'll find that you have less of a risk here, as these club members are more likely be to strong acquaintances rather than close friends or family.

Weddings and Parties

You may see the best version of someone else's hair at a wedding or party, because people have spent time on their hair to make it look it's best. They may be wearing special occasion hair which has been beautifully coiffed in an updo.

The style of the hair is featured in these instances, which means that time, money and product—or some combination of the three—have likely been invested in this beautiful finished look. However, it's crucial to remember that the haircut is only one component of the visual appeal of hair itself. The way hair is styled with its finished look, is as enticing as a beautifully wrapped wedding gift, in pretty paper and white bows. If the box is even in size and shape, and has been wrapped with special care, the wrapping paper is easier to fit on that foundation, and so the gift looks prettier. The same thing applies to haircuts and styles.

Wedding hair requires an extra effort for a picture-perfect day. If you are looking for a stylist to do wedding hair or special occasion hair at an upcoming event of your own, this is the ideal place to snag a referral for your special day. I strongly recommend this approach, if this is what you have in mind. Not all hairstylists are specialized in these areas, though. You would be surprised to know how many hairstylists don't know how to braid, cornrow or tease hair.

Certain skill-sets may be stronger in some areas than others. The salon's specific marketplace and environment, as well as the client demand for a specific trend, has a strong influence of how a certain skill-set develops over the course of a stylist's career.

What Should You Ask Someone Who Is Offering a Referral?

In your search for a new salon and stylist, here are some things to consider when asking for a referral.

- Why do they like a particular stylist? What do they look for in a stylist?

- What is the salon relationship like? Do they get along, or is it a relationship of tolerance?

- How long have they been seeing this particular stylist?

- Are they a reformed Chair Hopper?

- What do they like the most about this stylist's service? Is it primarily about the person or more about the hair itself?

- What do they like the least? Listen closely to this one!

- Is the service expensive? How much do they charge? Cost and value need to be considered here.

A Note About Pricing

I would like to draw attention to the last question about price, and raise more questions that many might overlook: How much *value* do they feel they receive in the appointment and service? Is it worth what they're paying? If so, why?

By asking about price this way, you will learn what is important to someone without putting them on the spot to disclose what they pay. Also, you can compare the value of the experience, and whether it is similar to yours. You can always call the salon for price specifications, or go to the salon website for that info.

I will say that it is very difficult for salons to offer exact quotes over the phone. In fact, at our salon we have a policy of *not* offering quotes over the phone. We have a guide on our website to give new clients an idea of how much their service will cost, and we will give estimates over the phone, but we won't offer an exact quote until the initial consultation. This is because clients may not communicate certain key pricing factors over the phone, especially if they are not clear about the service they need.

People call us for a price without understanding that we usually give a higher estimate over the phone, in an effort to protect ourselves from overpromising. Once we've have had the opportunity to make a full assessment at the consultation, the client's best service option is often much less expensive than their original phone inquiry.

A thorough consultation clears the fog for everyone. We are happy to give exact prices before we start our services, and will honor those prices even if more work is required than we originally thought. Not every salon does that, but many hairdressers I've worked with have honored their quotes. However, policies may differ in corporate and chain salons. I have never worked in that arena, and so I do not know the protocols. However, I have had people share experiences with me on both sides of the chair, and their accounts indicate that salon chains enforce much stricter policies in that area.

I can be more flexible because I am the salon owner, and I see each situation firsthand. Consequently, I have the authority to make these kinds of business decisions, and support the original quote. I must reiterate, however, that a quote is different from an estimate in my salon. An estimate is given over the phone, while a quote is offered at the consultation, in person.

It really all comes down to trust and communication.

We often get calls for price checks, and sometimes people quickly hang up on us. This is frustrating because we feel, if only we'd had more time, we would have been able to direct these inquiries to other, more economical alternatives—even if that means visiting a different salon. We understand and respect people's budgets and priorities, and simply want to help. There is enough business in this industry for anyone who is willing to offer *good service value.*

There is a barber shop on the other side of our parking lot that we refer business to, and we're happy to do so. I know of two friendly neighborhood barber shops that prefer not to offer complicated, long hair cuts or chemical services, and so they refer clients to us. We have other salons that we refer weddings and larger parties to as well.

We are a small specialty salon with a focus on corrective work and consultations. We specialize in women's hair, and we recognize that not all people need our type of service. Our unique niche emphasizes client communications and coaching in the salon industry. We are not a conventional salon.

This concept of specialties within a trade is relatable, especially in comparison to the example of deciding on which plumber to call. I have three brothers who are plumbers, and all three of them have plumbing businesses that cater to different aspects of the marketplace. One brother has a larger commercial business, another specializes in remodeling, and the third brother works primarily in new construction. They have all different niches, just as salons often salons do.

Decide what type of salon and specialty you need, and then book a consultation. The first consultation can be scheduled with your first hair appointment, especially if you want to avoid making two trips to the salon. We often do this for our clients.

Don't be afraid to ask for an exact quote at the consultation. As much as you want to feel like a princess when you leave the salon, your Hairy Godmother understands that the owners of the modern castle most likely have monthly mortgage payments, as well as payments for the four wheeled carriage that the princess rides in. We want you to enjoy your time at the salon without putting you in rags, and leaving you with no funds to go the ball.

Approaching the Salon Castle

There are many reasons why you may find yourself venturing into a new salon. It may be because of relocation, loss or dissatisfaction with your last hairdresser. For some, it can be a terrifying process, especially if they have suffered a hair trauma. You can find the source of these permanent scars in the gallows of childhood photos and high school yearbooks, as well as driver's license photos.

A great way to counteract any apprehension is to enter the salon and schedule a minimal service, such as a blow dry. This can be a quick and easy way to assess the salon environment without having to commit. In addition, it feels much more casual and non-committal than a haircut or color appointment.

You will feel less obligation if you decide to try another stylist on the next visit. It's similar to meeting for coffee instead of going out on an official first dinner date. The investment and obligation is much less in terms of both time and money.

Just Looking

If you prefer, just go on in to a salon and look over the retail products near the reception. Be sure to let the receptionist know why you are there. Not all salons have receptionists these days, so if there is no receptionist around, let a staff member or working hairdresser know that you recognize she is busy with a client, and that you do not want to intrude or take the time away from the person sitting in the salon chair.

Browsing the retail area is your best strategy when it comes to entering the *castle gates* while investing the least time and money. The best thing to do is to observe the area and others' interactions while keeping a low profile. However, there is no need to wear dark sunglasses and hide behind plants. Reassure salon staff that you just wanted to be sure about the location, and to browse through some products, and to possibly make an appointment for a blow dry or consultation. Any potential Hairy Godmother will already know that you are going to be a great guest in the castle! Your objective is to identify your potential Hairy Godmother and her working hours, as well as assess the environment she works in

Listen to the how business is conducted. Make a mental note of people on their way out the door and observe who looks the happiest. You may not like certain styles leaving in the castle, but not everyone wants to be a princess. The fact that people seem happy when leaving, is indicative that they are getting what they want.

If a stylist doesn't seem busy when you walk in, and you feel comfortable enough to schedule a shampoo/blow dry, ask for the next available appointment. Wait until *they* offer; sometimes a hairstylist may have just a few minutes for a bite to eat on a busy day, and even though they may not seem busy, this break could be their first of the day. Sometimes I don't get lunch until 4 o'clock. It's hard to say "no" to princesses.

Perhaps the timing works and feels right for you. If so, go for it right then and there. Remember to listen and to pay attention to their touch in the shampoo bowl. Don't skip the shampoo!

A great shampoo experience is a good sign that the stylist pays attention to detail. Avoid talking through your shampoo. You will learn a lot here by listening and paying attention. Don't be afraid to let the stylist know if you like a gentle or more vigorous shampoo, or if you prefer the water warmer or cooler.

After the shampoo, you will sit down at the styling station. It's important to note here that the goal is not to see whether they can blow dry your hair exactly as you'd like the first time, but rather, it is to determine whether they are attentive, personable, communicative and professional. If they meet that criteria, you can begin the journey of having your needs met consistently. Once you have established that you like the hairdresser, and you have taken the precautionary steps to feel safe, it's probably time to book that first haircut

On the day of the scheduled appointment, make a point to arrive early. Don't risk a rushed first appointment! Inform the receptionist that you are aware you're early, and that you arrived at the salon with time to spare to peruse the magazine selection. This will put everyone at ease. Again, keep a low profile, and observe your surroundings, including others' interactions. And don't forget to smile!

Castle Escape Plan

What if you didn't feel comfortable in there? Should you trust your gut and run for the door?

Yes!

No one has any information about you that is dangerous. You have the power and the right to walk away. Pick your moment by pretending you have an important phone call—and then step outside and leave! I have used that trick myself, at a nail salon earlier this year.

I am picky about nail salons. When I see clumping, half-empty polishes on the rack, I leave. I was out of town and waiting in a nail salon for the next available person to do my nails, and while in the waiting area I suddenly got a bad vibe. I stepped outside and pretended to make a phone call while the staff stared at me through salon the window. While pointing to the phone, I shrugged my shoulders and waved goodbye, while scrambling over to my car and letting them assume that I had an urgent obligation to attend to.

I was from out-of-state, so I felt confident that I'd never see them again. I know that sounds like a silly way of doing things, but I also know I'm not alone in this. Just a few weeks ago, a client walked into our salon and got spooked for some reason.

She had extreme anxiety and asked if we had any Benadryl. We didn't, and I probably wouldn't have given it to her if we had, due to the liability implications. We did, however, direct her to the nearest pharmacy, which was only one block away. She said she'd be back in just a few minutes, but we never saw her again. That mystery may never be solved.

Was Your First Date a Success?

I imagine that we all have stories of first dates both in and out of the salon. Aren't the similarities amazing? It's important to understand that dating and finding a great hairdresser, while they each have different objectives, both have similar methods. We often know right away whether we are going to click with someone, yet it doesn't always happen the way we expect.

And as for finding a great hairdresser, just like dating, it's a good idea to move slowly. Book the service when you feel ready, and enjoy a haircut or two before moving on to the next step, which is usually color. The advantage of this is you will have more opportunities to see the work of your stylist, and to learn the salon dynamics.

Not everyone will feel the need to be so cautious, and many people will just move from salon to salon, just as some jump from relationship to relationship in their lives. They may never be caught in the snares of the heartaches or bad burns from curling irons. In the end, you have to decide what approach is best for you.

Chapter 5

Invitation to the Ball

When Cinderella receives her invitation to the ball, she is both honored and excited. Suddenly, she becomes almost deflated when she realizes she has nothing to wear, and frantically worries over how she is going to look. Our modern- day princess faces similar pressures as she juggles the demands of her kingdom. There are many roles to manage in the modern castle, and the princess is often left with minimal resources in both time and money while preparing for special events.

A wedding, a funeral, a reunion or any other important event appear on the calendar and catch us of guard. An invitation to the ball can cause such panic, that the news can catapult a distressed princess over the salon castle walls, only to inadvertently invade the time slot of another salon princess sitting in the styling chair. This is so very awkward for your Hairy Godmother as she will then be faced with choosing to give more attention to one princess or the other. This is very upsetting for the princess who had already booked the appointment.

Sometimes an important date sneaks up on us as we race through our days believing we have ample time to prepare, only to find ourselves scrambling at the last minute. How can we prepare for things like this in advance?

Although the unexpected is always looming over us, we can ease some of the pressures by recognizing the rhythms in our lives. We can anticipate some of our needs and priorities ahead of time.

For example, consider preparing for a hurricane. We never know exactly when a hurricane may strike. Life in coastal South Carolina is wonderful, but we know that at certain times of year, it is wise to keep an array of essentials on-hand: batteries, bottled water, flashlights, candles and nonperishable food items are staples of preparedness to survive a potential hurricane. Having an evacuation plan, with a temporary place to stay in mind, and an emergency phone number preprogrammed into your phone, eliminates unnecessary panic.

Having a basic plan can offset franticness in all areas of life, and this is especially true when it comes to hair appointments. We know that the holidays are a busy time of year, and we can anticipate the rush. We know when New Year's is coming, as well as our anniversaries and birthdays. Even though we may not be able to see the details in advance, we can anticipate the timing of our haircuts and colors so that they accommodate these major events.

Desperate calls on New Year's Eve are often made to salons, frantic voices with last minute requests for extensive services like root colors and highlights. Staff and hours may be limited during these holiday vacation times, and so it's often difficult to find a salon castle that can offer the royal treatments a modern princess deserves.

Prescheduling may seem like too much of a hassle and pressure to some, but it can help eliminate the anxiety of trying to get a salon receptionist to *squeeze you in* right before an important day approaches.

Prescheduled appointments go hand in hand with successful consultations. They give both you and your stylist the time you need for effective collaboration and decision-making. Last-minute crises are breeding grounds for trouble and potential shortcuts (no pun intended). If possible, make your next appointment before you leave the salon. I can't say enough about the benefits of appointments, and the positive impact they have on the end result. You will feel much more empowered if you know you have set a specific time aside, just for you.

Another advantage is that you can begin to think about your goals, and start looking forward to your next appointment, especially if you decide you need to change your look. If you do have a change in mind, let your stylist know ahead of time, because it may mean that the stylist will need to schedule a longer appointment.

Your Hairy Godmother wants to give you her best, but unlike in the storybook, she needs a little more time to make the magic happen. The key is to find a stylist with a schedule that is consistently compatible with yours, and who is flexible, too.

In the dating world, sometimes, it may at times feel like all the good ones are taken. Don't be discouraged, though. Your Hairy Godmother is here for you!

Let's suppose you found the right salon, and the perfect stylist, and then you find she is not available for two months, and she can only see you during your work hours. Getting an appointment can be a major challenge. It can be worse than seeing a specialist doctor. There are clients that are very diligent in making their hair appointments, only to find themselves *squeezed in* among other clients. In addition, they may spend hours waiting for their chronically late hairdresser, and then when it *is* their turn, they are rushed through. What a fairytale nightmare!

The confidence to ask your hairdresser for something new, or to address an existing issue, is often diminished due to time constraints. Consequently, clients are often left with a choice to postpone an idea or issue until the following appointment. Sound familiar? It's even more common than you think.

It might be best to keep looking for another Hairy Godmother in this case, but there are other alternatives.

More Than One Hairy Godmother?

Remember, nothing says that you can't have two Hairy Godmothers. You could alternate appointments, and then always have a Hairy Godmother available when *you* need one.

I promise you that there are many great stylists out there who would be a wonderful match for you, and there is no law stating that you can have only one Hairy Godmother. I know of clients who visit one salon for haircuts and another for color services. The key is to prioritize open and respectful communication with everyone involved. It has to be understood that it's a personal preference, and that there is no hair police department that will bring you in for questioning. It's *your* decision to make. There is no shame. You *are* allowed two Hairy Godmothers.

I share joint custody with many stylists in other areas, and have even exchanged contact information with them so we can collaborate, especially with clients who migrate to the north in the summer. I welcome returning snowbirds who visit our warmer climate every winter, too.

I also have local clients who enjoy sitting in my salon chair, and yet are equally comfortable in the salon chair of my expert stylists, or other alternates with whom they have developed relationships.

Clients have established their very own relationships with my staff, and enjoy the team collaboration and benefits of a joint hair custody arrangement. We are delighted to have more flexibility with their constantly changing schedules.

Having a team of stylists who offer the same salon experience reduces anxiety for everyone concerned. It brings the best of both worlds to clients and hairdressers alike. The color formulas and products are more consistently used when kept in the same salon culture.

The clients' needs are easier to accommodate in this shared approach. Furthermore, clients don't feel stuck in a dependency, and stylists won't feel guilty if they have to go away. This also protects you from the fear of losing the one and only Hairy Godmother in your life.

When you find a salon kingdom with harmony and a team spirit, it truly is a wonderful thing. Appointments are more abundant, and everyone involved has a better chance of living happily ever after.

Pencil Me In

There are many approaches to prescheduling your appointments. Many salons use computers, while some still use the traditional pencil and paper appointment books. Each has their own unique advantages. A notebook with pencil and paper never locks up or freezes; it doesn't have computer glitches, and sometimes, can be far less frustrating than relying on technology.

I used the pencil and paper method for years, and when I transitioned into the digital world, I drove myself crazy carrying both an appointment book and a digital device because I didn't trust the safety and security of my information. It took me about three months to adapt, and it wasn't easy for me! I've been digital for thirteen years now, and I love my online and fully mobile business that I've built. As the business has grown, I have been able to process much more information, and more efficiently than ever before. Isn't technology wonderful? *Hmm,* I think the jury may still be out for some.

10 Steps to Better Booking

Look at your calendar before you pick up the phone. Even if you are booking your appointment online, this is helpful. Have two or three time slots in mind.

1. Keeps your calendar handy while you make your appointment, in case you need an alternate time. This will save time for both you and the receptionist.

2. Be clear and as specific as possible about your desired service. If you're not sure what service you need, schedule a brief consultation with your stylist just before your appointment.

3. If you want highlights with your base color, let them know so the time can be adjusted. If you change your mind about color, call ahead of time.

4. Allow enough time both before and after your appointment, so that you are not late and rushing your stylist. And don't forget to include the correct travel time!

5. Confirm the name of a new salon and confirm its location. Get directions, and do a test run if you're not sure how long the drive will take. This can save a lot of frustration on both sides of the salon chair, and keep you from arriving late. GPS is not always accurate, so don't rely solely on that. You may find you are across town in front of an empty lot, because your phone took you to the wrong location.

6. Decide how many weeks you want to have between appointments, and then prebook a time that is convenient for you. Your hair grows an average of a half-inch per month.

I have seen it grow much slower *and* much quicker, but your hair will grow. If you feel that after four weeks your hair is too long, it is a good idea to prebook an appointment for that week. You can always adjust the time if something comes up. Consult with your stylist if you need help making a decision.

7. Remember the receptionist is a liaison between you and your hairdresser. Don't shoot the messenger. She can give you advice, but she is not the one who will be working on your hair—so direct your questions and concerns to your stylist at the consultation. The receptionist is there for scheduling purposes, and to help you get the advice and services you need.

8. Busier clients have an even greater need to pre-book their appointments, as their calendars tend to be less flexible, and they are often caught off-guard in the event of any changes. The demands of the kingdom around us can overshadow the time we need to take care of ourselves. A hair appointment is an effective way to remind us that self-care is not only important, but essential. (I am guilty of this my-self)

9. If you are going to be late, please call ahead of time. Even five minutes can make a difference for your stylist. It may mean she can eat her lunch or return a phone call.

10. Plan your holiday appointments by looking ahead at when you're to going to be away, or when you're expecting company. If you don't know the exact days, then book times when you know you'll be free. Keep in mind, that just as the malls and parking lots fill up with holiday shoppers, so do salons.

Cancellations, Confirmations and No-Shows

Cancellations are expected in our business. Call as soon as you know you're no longer able to make your appointment. No matter how late you are in cancelling, it truly can make a difference for someone else. It's a good idea to follow up with an e-mail or text if it's really short notice. I don't charge for cancellations, but if they are excessive and frequently last-minute, I will be cautious of rebooking that client. If it happens out of circumstance rather than of character of habit, I will rebook the appointment at the end of the day so that if they cancel, I can simply go home early. If it happens out of habit rather than of circumstance, I will give a friendly last chance warning, and then decline to rebook the appointment.

Our salon sends confirmations via email a couple of days before each scheduled appointment. It's a good idea, if there is an opportunity, to respond to a confirmation, especially if your salon requests it. We call them confirmations rather than reminders, so that we can confirm any change in the service. Some clients may say they want to keep the appointment time, but that they would prefer to keep the color service and postpone their haircut.

Confirmation emails are a great opportunity to announce new ideas and any possible changes. Our clients email us pictures from their phones of all potential new looks they're considering, which is a wonderful way for us to prepare for the consultation.

We rarely have no-shows. No-shows are different than cancellations, and they are absolutely forgivable—that is, if they are not habitual. It is inevitable that in life, some unforeseen emergencies arise.

If they are illegitimate emergencies, or deliberate acts, born of a pattern of negligence, then this is very disrespectful to the stylist. A hairstylist's time is irreplaceable; it is the lifeblood of the business. Missed appointments, mean missed revenue and opportunities. Time cannot be replaced.

The same rules and consideration apply to your time. If a hairdresser has ever left you waiting, or if she was a no show, I apologize on her behalf.

If it's happening a lot, then you deserve better. Too many cancelations mean that she is definitely not your Hairy Godmother. Life happens, and nobody's perfect; and we all make mistakes, myself included. Everyone's time is important, and it took me years to understand that. Let me share one of the biggest lessons I learned on that regard:

The Most Torturous Squeeze

About fifteen years ago, I learned a valuable life lesson from one of my dearest friends in the whole world. Her name is Dawnne, and we met in church. It was a sizable congregation, and yet it had the warmth of a little country church, and it felt to me like the *Little House on the Prairie*. This church was indeed a second family to me.

Dawnne and I grew to be fast friends, and I am still blessed to call her my friend after seventeen years of life events including births, deaths and marriages. We had many things in common, both then and now. For example, we share the same birthday, family responsibilities, kids and a heart that loves good coffee and humor. She also had a close connection to the salon industry, as her mom was also a hairdresser in a neighboring state. Not long into our friendship, I became Dawnne's honorary hairdresser. I felt a deep responsibility for my friend and her styling needs.

We were both tight on funds, and I felt I could help her by offering salon services free of charge. Sounds great, right? Dawnne always offered to pay, but I refused. She was my dear friend and I wanted to help her. I loved doing her hair, and besides, it didn't feel like work to me. I didn't feel right taking her money. The problem was that I could only afford to do Dawnne's hair when I didn't have *paying clients* on the schedule. If a paying customer walked in, or booked an appointment for the time I'd set aside for Dawnne, I was notorious for simply being unable to say "no", and so I would "squeeze" people in and over overbook myself instead. Dawnne would be left waiting, but she was my friend. Besides, she didn't mind because she didn't have to pay, right? Wrong!

This went on for about a year or so until one day, I noticed that Dawnne had a new look—and that it hadn't come from me. When I asked her about it, she said that she was desperate, and got it done on a whim somewhere else. It was a little awkward at first, and I half-believed her story until I found out that she had gone to see another hairdresser in our church, who worked on the other side of town. She clearly didn't just drop by on impulse. My mind started to race as this sense of betrayal hit me. I realized she'd been declining my offers for weeks, saying she was too busy to schedule an appointment, when in fact she was giving me the "artful dodge." Needless to say, I was crushed. I questioned myself on so many levels, and wondered who had won her business. How could she possibly not have wanted to come to me anymore when I was free? Was I so lousy that she would rather pay someone than sit in my chair? Unbelievable! The more I thought about it, the more it bothered me, until finally I decided to confront her. I decided to call her on the phone. Dawnne was much more passive back then, and avoided confrontation at all costs. I was the opposite. I called her, practically shaking with emotion, and asked what I had done wrong. She sighed and said, "Well, I'm sorry, but I wanted to be treated like a real client."

I was confused. Dawnne explained that she loved my work, regardless of the fact that I was her friend. She said she wanted the client experience in the salon and was willing to pay for it, but I kept refusing her money. She felt she had no choice. I just didn't hear what she was saying. Dawnne was one of my very best friends, and I hadn't listened to her. I felt awful about it, but knew that she was right. I learned a very valuable lesson that day, and I am so grateful that my friend was brave enough to tell me: I learned that listening and valuing everyone who sits in my chair is of the utmost importance, regardless of who they are. My friend saw how others were being treated and wanted the princess treatment for herself, too, but I had inadvertently denied her that experience.

She still visits my salon from time to time, even though as we live in different towns now. Still, I am absolutely committed to giving her my full attention and service. We enjoy our time in the salon and visit, and instead of paying—she buys dinner.

If you are in a situation like this, whether you are the stylist or the friend, it's worth having a conversation. It's risky, but real friends will work it out. I treasure my dear friend Dawnne, and I want to thank her again for saving me from myself.

Surprises for Hairy Godmothers

Some days don't go so smoothly for whatever reason, and sometimes the timing is just off, even though you may have gone to a great salon with fantastic stylists. All I can say is that nobody's perfect, and that things do not always go according to plan. Don't immediately dismiss someone for mitigating circumstances.

An unexpected event occurred and just so happened that it was on the first appointment of someone who had been referred to me. If I'd have been in her shoes, I might have run, but for whatever reason, she didn't— Here is her story:

The Awesome Amanda Tale

The day seemed like it was going to be a normal one for me. I had a new client scheduled for a foil highlight. Her name was Amanda, and she had booked the appointment by phone after she received a strong recommendation from one of my son's old high school buddies, who just happened to be her coworker.

She arrived on time, only to find me dashing frantically toward the salon door. I almost ran her over as she was walking in.

"I am so sorry. You must be Amanda?" I blurted, and continued speaking rapidly, not unlike a farm auctioneer. "I wonder if you could give me about twenty minutes or so? My potential daughter-in law has just called to inform me that a deer ran out just now while she was driving and wrecked her car! She's fine, but a little shaken and asked me to stay with her until the cops arrive. She is literally just two miles down the road. I just need to get to her. Will that be okay? Or would you prefer to reschedule? I think I'll still be able to do your hair. I just need about twenty minutes; I'll still have time if you do? I know you were looking forward to your appointment. Everything should be fine. What do you think?"

I was still talking at warp speed as Amanda followed me outside and watched me climb into my minivan. I was in mom mode, and in my mom mobile. This beautiful young blonde waved and nodded in support, as though I were setting sail onboard a Naval Ship, leaving the harbor. She said she would wait for me.

Who does that? What would you have done? Run out the door, right?

This darling young woman waited. I returned as I said I would, after about twenty-five minutes. She was so kind and concerned. All I can say is that must have been some recommendation! Or maybe she just had a good vibe?

I may have run if I'd been in her shoes, but for whatever reason, Amanda stuck around, and I am sure glad she did. Despite the craziness of the day, I still took time to consult with her, and gave her the high-lift contrasted blonde hair that she asked for, and of course at a discounted price in an attempt to compensate for her compassion and understanding. Amanda has been with me for almost seven years now; she is a married mother two cute little kids. She is a hardworking, loving, giving, and someone I would be proud to have as a daughter. I often tell her that she would be a great hairdresser because she has the exact kind of compassionate heart we need in the profession. I would love for her to join my team. She is truly awesome!

Walk-ins and Waiting

I have spent a solid chunk of this chapter discussing the value of prescheduled appointments, but I must offer special acknowledgement to walk-in salons. I want to convey that just because a salon accepts walk-ins, doesn't mean that the quality of their work is subpar, as some might conclude. It just means that you can agree to the risk of a wait in exchange for the freedom of not having to commit to a scheduled appointment.

My salon is a specialty salon with a focus on corrective color and cutting, both of which would conflict with a walk-in environment. We are a smaller, studio salon, so walk-ins are not recommended, but they are welcome if the timing allows.

Walk-in salons offer a vital service in our industry, and I applaud them for it. Great cuts and color can come out of these salons. The essence of any great cut and color service is rooted in the success of the communication in the consultation. I have hired some of my best stylists from walk-in salons, as they are fast and efficient, and well-practiced in the art of cutting hair. Walk-ins can be a gamble as far as the wait time goes, and walk-in clients may not have the opportunity to choose their stylist.

One advantage of walk-ins is that a longer wait time will give you the opportunity to observe the potential stylist at work before you take a seat in the salon chair. The problem is that if she is good, you will probably have to wait for your turn each time. Smartphones tend to make the pass more quickly.

Chapter 6

The Spellbinding First Cut

I hope that by this time in our journey together, you feel like there is hope. You are well on your way to breaking free from the dungeons and tortures of hair disasters. By now, you should realize that one of the most critical components of a successful haircut is taking the time for a consultation, and preparing for your appointments. The benefits from this are exponential, and will reduce the risk of unpleasant salon chair experiences and salon trauma.

You will learn a lot from the first cut with a qualified hairdresser. The first haircut is a strong indicator of how things will progress in the future. However, it's not just the technical side of the haircut that counts. We've explored who is looking in the mirror with us, and we now recognize that the source of our true reflection, prior to the appointment, affects who and what we see when we leaving. Let's delve deeper into the issue and take a look at how haircuts suit the individual, including the specific head shape that it sits on.

Haircuts are regular shapes that are fitted to irregular shaped heads. The combinations of angles can vary in many cases to achieve a specific haircut shape. Often, the haircut itself must be adapted to fit a specific head shape or hair texture. Some heads are flatter at the crown than others, and some have sharper curves at the nape of the neck. Hairlines and profiles are all different, and clients have various textures and styling capabilities. Your Hairy Godmother has to find the right combination for your lifestyle and personal expression, and that will match your time commitment and budget to achieve it. In a nutshell, Your Hairy Godmother is a perception and communications expert, with an understanding in human nature and geometrics.

The Good, the Bad and the Ugly Haircut Dilemma

There is a misconception about what distinguishes a good haircut from a bad one. Hairdressers see the matter differently than clients. Clients will often come in and say, "I want something that looks nice," or, "I just want a good cut."

But what do the words *nice* and *good* mean? These vague words, and the mental picture attached to them, are very different for everyone. Consultations will help decipher this and so should be set in a way that both parties commit their attention fully. There is a huge difference between hearing someone as compared to understanding what they're saying. Words can be misleading. It's not what you say — it's what others hear that counts.

I have my own definition of what a good cut is, based on my experience and training. This definition is the technical foundation for every haircut that takes place in my salon. Stylists who have adopted this, or a similar concept, truly understand the mechanics of haircutting.

*"A good haircut is one that fits the head shape, with
the correct length, volume and distribution of weight
throughout the hair, according to the individual style
needs of that particular client."*

Michelle Casey

The consultation is the starting point to achieving a great
haircut. Effective communication serves as an open
channel for the accurate exchange of information. More
often than not in a salon, communication is snagged
in the hooks of misinterpretation, time constraints and
distractions. Often, if the process is handled carelessly,
or if it's rushed, vital information may be over looked.
A keyword can be latched on to or even missed
completely, leaving the other vital informative words to
fall from the Cliffs of Caution, in to a sea of confusion,
only to be buried at the bottom of a hair disaster.

It's important to understand that a grasp of realistic
expectations should resonate with those on *both* sides
of the chair. Hair stylists have convinced clients of
what will they think will look good on a client without
considering the implication of the client's perception
and how she *feels* about the style and maintenance. Here
is an example:

Rita and the Magic New York Makeover

Rita has been my client for over four years now, and she
is a delight. She is in amazing shape for a woman in her
seventies, dressing very well and spends a lot of time on
the tennis court. She wears her hair in a caramel blonde
shade, with brighter highlights framing her petite face,

emphasizing her dark blue eyes and bright smile. Her hair length barely grazes her shoulders and she enjoys the option of pulling it back on the hot summer tennis courts. She is always so appreciative of everything I do and offers words of praise throughout her entire appointment. She loves hairdressers and salons, and is always open to new ideas.

Two years ago, Rita was visiting her daughter in New York City for the holidays. She received a warm welcome from her daughter, who surprised her with an appointment at a high-end salon. Rita was both honored and excited to see what magic they could work for her. The salon was amazing, and the grand finale of her fabulous spa-like experience was the much-anticipated haircut and style. The enthusiastic stylist looked at Rita and said, "We're going to make you look fabulous! Would you like me to do something that makes you look twenty years younger?"

Rita's eyes brightened with childlike excitement, and she said, "Sure!" She believed that she was safe in the hands of such an obvious professional. After all, she thought, he surely wouldn't have worked in such a sophisticated place if he wasn't good, right?

Well, what do you think happened? Rita was in for a shock! A short, sassy haircut, shaped perfectly into a very stylish wedge, tapered closely at the back to her beautiful slim neckline. It was a *technically* perfect cut, and it flattered her soft profile. As lovely as she looked, however, Rita felt *stunned* rather than *stunning*.

She was still in shock when she got home. She called me right away and told me what had happened. Rita explained to me that she wouldn't be in for a while, and that she needed to push back her next hair appointment, as she wanted to grow her hair back immediately. She said, "Wait 'til you see it, Michelle. It looks just terrible!"

Her husband hated it too, which only confirmed her belief that her haircut was a disaster. Rita felt terrible about the whole ordeal.

After a couple of months, Rita found herself back in my salon chair. Rita usually visits me about once every seven weeks, as her hair grows slower than the average person's. I thought the haircut still looked great. She said that it had grown some, and that she was feeling a little better, but that she was still reeling from her experience. She still had a residual look of dismay when she sat in front of the mirror and asked, "Who would ever say 'no' to looking twenty years younger? Why did he ask me that silly question? Of course I want to look twenty years younger — who doesn't? But if he had told me what that would have entailed, I would have said 'no, thanks!'"

After our discussion, she became more accepting of her situation and added, "Oh well, lesson learned. At least it will grow again." She sighed, looking up at me from the chair. "How long do you think it will take to grow back, Michelle?" I sighed too. Then, softening my voice, I replied as gently as I could: "About nine months."

Clients are the ones facing the daily hair horrors of these drastic hair change decisions. Even though it's great to be open to new ideas, they are often cloaked in confusing perceptions of what things *really are* and what things *should be*. The same thing applies to when we look in the mirror with our hairstylist.

Clients may simply ask for "a good haircut," and describe it as "short, with no fuss."

Careful listeners may be able to discern that the client believes a shorter cut will be easier to take care of. In fact, that's not always the case. Not only do shorter haircuts require much more frequent visits to the salon to maintain the shape, but the wrong short shape on a head is very frustrating for a client who is constantly struggling to create lift and volume in places where the hair has a tendency to collapse. In these cases, the hair simply doesn't seem to fit the head. There is no option to pin up short hair when you're in a hurry, and short hair often requires more frequent shampoos — sometimes even daily shampoos — in order to look fresh. Clients will wear hats in order to disguise a bad hair day, but many don't like wearing them. Typically, stylists will ask, "So, you would like me to cut it shorter?" instead of, "What do you like about short hair?" or "Why do you want short hair?"

Paying attention to these questions could reveal an entirely different set of answers and reveal greater needs with a higher priority. There is often too much assumption which is limiting possibility.

Clients will often ask for bangs thinking it will keep their hair out of their face, when in fact they may struggle more. Some may even choose to eliminate bangs as an option altogether, because they may picture a certain type of bang they dislike, or recall a bad experience with bangs. There are so many variations in bangs, and if a person makes the wrong decision, bangs will become a focal point for bad haircut flashbacks.

Layers are another misconception, as some clients believe they cause a butchered look, or that layers will make their hair look to "poofy", or perhaps thinner. Some clients almost recoil at the very thought of layers as I've seen the expression on someone's face change when they're recalling a throwback image of short ugly layers. Clients will opt for a style thinking that it will make their faces look thinner, or that it could minimize a large forehead or nose, and so they may choose a certain style or length because it looks easier to manage. These are all examples of clients' preconceived ideas. However, the stylist must discern and verify the strength of their client's beliefs and concerns to identify their best option.

A client's truth has been tailored by perception. Our perceptions are our own truth — our personal reality of what we see in the mirror. The questions that need to be asked are a hybrid of *what, why* and *which and how.* Here are the main questions we ask in our salon:

- What do you like?

- What is the most important thing about your hair?

- Why do you think this is a good choice
  for you?

- Which picture do you prefer, and why?

- Which picture is closest to what you like?

- How much time are you willing to invest to
  maintain the look?

Sometimes things can still be overlooked, but with consistency in our communication, a solution will surely emerge. As much as I pride myself on my commitment to actively listen, I still have the elusive case here and there, where I have totally missed a vital piece of information. Here is a prime example:

Shine on Sharon

Sharon is a current client of mine from South Africa. It's hard to keep a straight face when I am around her because she is just so darned funny! She is a gorgeous Asian lady, in her late fifties, with a very slender build. She wins awards in both golf and tennis, and she is an avid swimmer. Consequently, Sharon chooses to wear her hair medium-length, with a layered look. The naturally dark hair she once knew now requires color touchups every three to four weeks, so I see Sharon quite often. Together, our accents spark a special breed of puzzled looks at the salon, especially when consulting together. I just don't know how we do it sometimes; maybe it is because we laugh our way through all the confusion until we get to the clearing. and we don't give up!

One day Sharon came in with something specific in mind regarding her hair. She was showing me quite a number of pictures that appeared to be all over the place with different looks. None seemed to have anything in common with the rest. In short, I noted that Sharon was choosing completely different haircuts, moving from layered cuts to one length, and looking at both shorter and longer looks. I was so confused! I honestly thought she was thinking out loud about her options, and that she really had no idea of what she wanted. She was becoming a little strained with me, recognizing that I was still clueless. It finally dawned on me to ask this simple question: "What specifically do you like about that picture?" Sharon answered, "See how shiny and healthy it looks? I love the shine." I pointed to another picture and asked the same thing — and I got the same answer! Shine. She wanted shine! We looked at each other as if the enigma code had just been broken. Finally, I understood.

We scheduled a gloss color and Sharon loved it. Fortunately, she did like her haircuts, and so that explains why she didn't give up on me.

Clients' Spells and Incantations

When clients attempt to describe their hair, the situation can be both puzzling and comical. It can be as delightful as deciphering a toddler's strange new words. In fact, an auto mechanic is the only other person I can think of who may get a variety of comical sounds coming from customers who are trying to diagnose their ailing engines. Accounts of clunks and tapping reenacted with hissing and knocking sounds must be hilarious to watch, while a mechanic attempts to discern these common noises. I don't get as many sounds as mechanics, but I do see plenty of animated gestures and facial expressions with strange words. Consultations are not always painful — they can be hilarious. I treasure these words and what they mean to the individuals who have shared them. Here are a few examples:

- "Hairanoia": This self-diagnosis was coined by Lynn, one of our clients, who called and said her hair was getting on her nerves, and that she needed an appointment ASAP.

- "Tossed Salad": Ellie's name for her blow drying technique, which involves drying the hair with no brush, using the hands in a salad-tossing motion.

- "Muchy": From an out of town client. This is still a mystery, but we think it means a more graduated bob, with less bulk.

Taking the Mystery Out of the Magic

It is my job to identify the key words a client uses consistently to interpret the most dominant self-expressions. These keywords help me decide the client's highest priority so that I can create options for her to choose from. I boil down the overwhelming number of choices to the best options which simplifies the process, and helps avoid confusion. I will filter the information down to three comparative options, with pictures, and go from there. Up until recently, I used hair magazines, but now I rely more on digital images, as it seems faster to run a search. The first thing I do in a consultation is explain the basic concepts of hair.

We address haircuts in three dimensions:

1. Length: We ask the client to focus on the length first.

2. Weight: We ask the client to show us where their hair feels too heavy or bulky on their head.

3. Volume: Then we ask where would she like more lift and volume.

These steps simplify the process of sifting through endless pictures of dead-end images, raising anxiety levels as the clock ticks.

It is often poorly distributed weight lines in the haircut causing problems, for many clients, with styling regimes. We address the weight in the hair by educating our clients about these basic principles. Clients often state that their hair is too long, when they actually mean it's too *heavy* in places. Communication is the foundation of our success in the salon, as we have simplified the process for clients to identify and communicate their needs. A stylist can quickly target the client's main areas of concern and perform the haircut in a timely fashion. A common language empowers both clients and stylists to work as a team.

The Salon Castle Keys

The keys to effective communication in the salon are not just in the words, but also in the intent and structure of the communication. Marriage counselors cannot help a marriage unless both parties are willing to set aside their feelings and work toward a solution, and back it with a time commitment. The same concept applies in the salon environment. Here are a few things to consider to help build a platform of successful salon communication:

1. Clients need to identify a stylist with whom they feel comfortable.

2. Professionals need systemized communications with a common language and terms to empower both the client and the stylist.

3. Both the client and the stylist should honor time for the consultation with each and every appointment.

4. Commit to a team effort and respectful communication.

These are the fundamentals that will lead to lasting and consistent results. It is both a practice and an evolving process built on a foundation of trust and respect. This is truly where magic begins!

Haircut and Style Confusion

Some clients look through magazines and pictures, and believe that the model's haircut is the primary contribution to achieving those photo finished looks. It's important to take in to consideration that styling techniques, as well as the products used, affect the end result. It goes without saying that a camera ready pose, staged with arranged lighting to enhance shiny hair, jewelry, make-up and wardrobe serve as major components to the pleasing looks of models. These are huge factors that affect the perception of the haircut.

Robert Cromeans, Global Artistic Director for John Paul Mitchell Systems, frequently states the following phrase, which is a philosophy that I have incorporated into my own salon culture:

The Cut Creates the Shape,
Style Creates Finish.

Clients are often disappointed because they are confused by this concept. I have seen many clients come into my salon distressed over a bad haircut, when the real culprit is actually styling.

We can change the entire look of the original haircut, much like interior decoration makes or breaks a room. A good haircut is like the basic four walls of a room; selecting different types of lighting, and furniture with either neutral or bold-colored walls, will affect the entire feel of the room. It is the same with hair, and the effects of styling and color selection.

When frustration occurs as a result of this confusion, sometimes the client's only option is to abandon ship and go to another stylist. The client may request a" new" haircut from the new stylist and receive the very same cut. Clients become baffled as to why hairstylists won't listen to them, and find that every new stylist they meet seems to give them the same haircut, instead of targeting the perceived *style*. This makes clients question the whole salon experience. In turn, hairdressers who experience this assume that the client will never be happy and stop trying to satisfy their needs. Sounds like a troubled marriage, doesn't it?

Clients feel like nobody "gets it," not to mention stuck and frustrated. When the client looks at her reflection in the mirror at the end of her appointment, and struggles to conceal her obvious disappointment, stylist's puzzled heads shake and frustrations build because her hair just does not look right. The stylist gave them what they asked for, but not what they really wanted.

Sometimes the issue is about more than just communication — sometimes technical issues are involved. As much as I hate to admit it, technical problems and inexperience go hand in hand. How do you know if you have the right person cutting your hair? Online reviews make it much easier to assess the hairdresser's performance, not to mention the kind of experience you will encounter in the salon chair, but it doesn't always reveal the stylist's level of experience. You have probably done your homework, and so you have likely avoided the following scenario, and still you may have found yourself unknowingly in a rookie's chair. Nothing against rookies though, because I was once a rookie myself; I have never forgotten that horrific experience.

The Queen of England Tale

Let me take you back to 1990, to my first week working in a posh salon. I was found cowering in the backroom, which was also known as the dispensary. This room was where hairdressers mixed their magic potions and kept their secrets. I was hiding there because I was dreading the call from up front to perform a haircut on the first client of my new career.

I had been hired straight out of beauty school because due to the potential I'd apparently revealed in interview, and also because I was an affordable investment at a $125 flat rate each week, plus tips. I had completed 1,500 hours of training in beauty school, working with a combination of mannequins and economically-enticed beauty school clients. I had passed the South Carolina state board exam with flying colors, and still, with all my qualifications, I wasn't ready to face my first client. It was my first *real* paying client, in a real salon.

I was terrified because I was responsible for both the haircut and style. I would either kick off my reputation as a new hairdresser with a bang, or a big black mark would go down on my record as a defining shame. Many hairdressers have faced this same situation and the latter is much more common. We are often thrown to the wolves early in our career which partly explains the dropout rate.

I had to give off the impression that I knew what I was doing, when in fact I was still very uncertain. Anyone could walk through that salon door. They could ask for anything, and I had to be ready and know how to do it. Few, if any, beauty salons in my area offered official "in-salon" training programs, although many mall chains and corporate salons did. During that time, my focus was on the drawbacks of the hourly rates and the late working hours of a mall salon. As a new mom, I wanted to be in control of my own schedule. My husband only had Sundays off, so I couldn't even work half-days on Saturdays. Plus, I also worried that I would be in a cookie-cutter environment, and felt that I would be limited in creative ways. I feared that I would be stuck in an assembly line, or perhaps I'd get fired for being so slow and lacking in confidence. I didn't even apply for a job at those places, which, in hindsight, may have been bit hasty.

I was a much more limited thinker in those early years. The truth is that after I graduated from cosmetology school, it was up to me to further my education and improve my skills. Choosing a good salon was essential when it came to surviving the first two years of my career. There was no YouTube back then; it was all on-the-job training. I coped by covertly watching the more experienced stylists, asking questions whenever I could in the backroom. My main goal was to hide my inexperience from clients. I mean, who would want to sit in the chair of a nervous rookie, performing the first unsupervised haircut and then be expected to pay full price for the service? Do you think you have ever been that client? How would you know for sure? How do hairdressers gain experience when they have no experience, if the salon doesn't offer training? I had practiced many times on family members, but they knew the deal — I cut for free, so no guarantee. It was a terribly unnerving time for me. I am so glad those days are behind me.

Finally, I was called up to the front. My elderly client sat down in the reception, unaware of my fear. *Lord deliver me*, I thought. I braved my way over to greet her, faking a confident smile, and pretending to know more than I did. I desperately hoped that my lack of experience would go unnoticed.

"Hi. I'm Michelle. I'm going to be taking care of you today. Would you like to come this way?" I gestured with my hand, escorting her to the salon chair. I was still trying not to grimace, through my fake smile. My client nodded, gripping her posh handbag, and took a seat in the salon chair. She continued to clutch her bag and stared sternly into the mirror. Recognizing that she was serious about getting down to business, I asked the next obvious question.

"So, what can I do for you today?"

"Well," she began "I would like it tidied up a bit, please".

She had a British accent! What wonderful luck — I have one of those too. I was sure that would lighten things up a bit. Instant connection and reprieve, or so I thought.

"Oh you're British! So am I!" I said enthusiastically.

"Really?" She looked up, her eyes suspicious, and inquired, "What part?"

"Oh" I replied, "I'm from Nottingham!" Still smiling—almost giddily.

The woman, however, turned her nose up and stared back in to the mirror at her reflection. "Hmmm...A Place one would rather pass through don't you think?"

she remarked rudely, not unlike the Dowager Duchess from *Downton Abbey*.

What could I say to that? I tried not to appear stunned, and so I simply said, "Yes. I suppose." I was even more uncomfortable than I had previously thought possible. I knew I couldn't show it, and so I added, "And so what part of England are you from?"

"Surrey. I'm here on holiday with my daughter and she will be coming to pick me up soon. How long do you think all this will this take?"

By then, I knew I was doomed. *Great, here I am with no real experience, and with an English sourpuss, and now I'm racing a clock.* Everyone in beauty school knew I was the slowest. How much worse could it get? I had to keep my cool. Still smiling, I calmly said, "Oh, not too long, I hope. You just need me to tidy it up with a light trim, right? How would you like it styled?"

My client cupped the side of her hair with her hands and gestured as she spoke. "I would like it set and curled neatly, and styled away from my face, brushed back and coiffed on top with some poof." She continued, "I like it styled like... like...." She hesitated just slightly, and then continued, "Well, you're British! You should know... like the Queen's hair!"

Her shrill voice echoed in my ears, as I tried to make sense of how I was going to achieve this magic trick on a woman with such fine hair. Keeping my composure, I blurted out, "Of course!" Then I suggested, "We should perhaps get started then, and head over to the shampoo bowl."

I led the way, making a conscious effort not to shake my head in disbelief. How could I possibly do this? Did she really want to look like the Queen of England, or just to have hair like the Queen? Who knew? Either way, I knew neither was going to happen. Of all the people in the world, this lady landed in my chair on my very first day of work. I was a wreck. What was I going to do? I decided that I had to make the best of it and simply face the consequences. As I was shampooing the old dear's hair, I started to contemplate my approach.

In a sense, thinking about the technicality of the haircut left me relieved. The woman had a simple, uniform haircut. It was a beauty school standard cut, and a no-brainer, except that I was still quite slow. The roller set would also take extra time, and I was even slower at that, but I knew the basics. Panic and frustration crept in again as I strategized my plan. Who wore roller sets in 1990, anyway? I wanted to do fun, pretty hair. This wasn't what I'd signed up for! Nevertheless, I had a job to do. I pulled myself out of an emotional nosedive and decided to focus on just getting through the appointment.

After the shampoo, I remembered to preheat a hood dryer, and by then I'd managed to steady myself by tuning out both the internal and external chatter. The lady seemed less annoyed when I stopped talking. I rolled her hair and placed her under the dryer for twenty minutes. I took the opportunity to step into the backroom and gather myself before the dreaded comb-out. That was going to be the tricky part for me, especially since I knew this woman was going to be picky.

The drying time flew by, and I soon found myself back at the styling chair, pulling out my client's rollers. At least she wasn't tender-headed. I began teasing the top of her hair.

My many years of experience have taught me that I did not use enough of the right products to support the woman's fine hair. As a result, her hair was too soft, and so the base tease wasn't firm enough. It deflated like a soufflé with too many sinkholes. I kept going over it, trying to make it smoother and more finished, but it just looked like a nest. My first client's hair was a disaster. I tried to comb it a second time, and tidy it up more by teasing it again. Finally, it started to take shape and look better, but by then the lady was "on to me" and was just sitting there staring in disgust. I, in turn, had become red in the face, and I'd broken out in a nervous sweat. It was horrifying. And then suddenly, an attractive blonde in her forties arrived, exuding eagerness and positivity. It was the daughter who had come to retrieve her mother. I really began to panic then, well aware of the fact that my time was up and I had yet to finish my client's hair.

She greeted her elderly mother and asked in the kindest voice, "How's it going, Mummy?"

Her mother responded both angrily and woefully "Not very well I'm afraid."

"Why, whatever is wrong, Mummy?"

With an immediate reply, the woman's words were sharp. "It's too flat on top and it doesn't have any puff."

The daughter tried to cheer her again. "Perhaps if she teases it a little more, Mummy"

"I've already asked her to do that and apparently she's not very good at it."

It was as if I were an invisible servant in the room. The lady continued with her complaints in front of everyone in the salon, including other clients. She groaned loudly and finally said, "I've had quite enough of this. Just stop now, please. I will just have to make do with it as it is."

I knew there was no consoling her, despite my apologies. I knew I had failed to give her what she wanted, and I knew it was my fault. I could try to blame it on the hair, but other hairdressers had surely made her happy in the past. Right? I do remember exchanging a knowing glance with her daughter, and it appeared that she'd expressed compassion for me. In fact, I got the impression that this was not the first time she had seen this scene with her mum. Or maybe I had just told that to myself to make the memory less painful. Who knows?

The point of the story is simply to offer another perspective, from a hairstylist's point of view. I was an inexperienced stylist, young and immature in many ways, but I was still a person with feelings. My first client was definitely rude, and perhaps unrealistic. You might say that neither of us benefited from the experience. I believe that as horrific as it was to start my career in that way, I learned from my first client. I learned who I did not want to work with, and I learned that I needed to learn how to attract a clientele I wanted to keep.

Questions For Magical Styles

As we consider the ways in which we style hair, we must understand that we can completely disguise the haircut. These are some questions to consider when you consider a particular style:

1. How much time are you willing to spend styling your hair (minutes)?

2. How often are you willing to spend time on your hair each day (frequency)?

3. What are your styling skills? Do you use a blow-dryer or styling tool?

4. Do you like to wear your hair both up and down?

5. Do you wear your hair the same way most of the time?

6. Do you embrace change?

7. Do you prioritize how your hair feels over how it looks? Or the opposite? This is very important when it comes to styling options and product use.

8. Do you like the texture of your hair?

9. How often do you want to visit the salon for maintenance cuts?

10. How much are you willing to invest in the recommendations of a qualified stylist? Oftentimes, people will forfeit quality for economy. What is your priority?

A thorough discussion about your precious locks can be overwhelming for both you and the stylist. One appointment is not enough time to cover the big picture, especially when there is no compass to navigate the conversation in any particular way, which puts the stylist's schedule at risk. Stylists are looking for efficient ways to help you find what you need. So where do we go from here? Simple: We get realistic about expectations for immediate solutions and start building a strategy.

Perhaps if we understand that finding the right personality and building a relationship on trust is the first step. This is the foundation for us to move forward, to collaborate and to create a more realistic environment. Both personal and professional relationships take time to build, no matter how skilled a person is. The same thing applies to your Hairy Godmother.

Here are some tips to help you prepare for your consultation, especially when it comes to describing your hair to your stylist.

- Think about your ideal end result ahead of time, including why it is important to you. Bring two or three pictures of your hair when you *liked* the cut and style. Point out the specific feature you enjoyed.

- Save time by describing what you *want* instead of what you don't want.

- Don't take big risks unless you know your stylist well or you are sure of the person performing the service.

- If you feel that you need more time for your
  consultation, schedule a meeting before
  the haircut.

- If the first haircut is close to what you want,
  but not quite there, hang in there. If you have
  a good rapport with the stylist, it's worth
  sticking around to iron out the kinks. If the
  communication is solution-oriented on both
  sides, it is less threatening.

Digging for answers prior to taking a seat in the salon
chair could save a lot of grief. Going the extra mile
will hopefully help you build a respectful relationship
with the right stylist, and bring about consistent results.
Not every stylist is committed to great service, but
most of us are in the business to serve people, and to
help them feel good about themselves. It's fun being a
Hairy Godmother when you are working with people
who appreciate you. And in return, a Hairy Godmother
should always appreciate the journey of her Queens
and Princesses.

Home Haircut Disasters

I have had many clients give me their accounts of when
they attempted to cut their own hair. I have even had a
dear client, named Colleen, who sent me a selfie. She
posed in front of the bathroom mirror, with her bangs
held hostage between the blades of household scissors.
The words *Help Me!* were the only words written in
the caption. This was a fashion emergency, and so I
responded with our salon equivalent of a 911 call, and
talked her down from the ledge. She was able to get an

appointment within the hour that day. I can't always do that, though. It really depends on my schedule, not to mention the client's.

Many people apologize to me for their attempts at trimming their own bangs, or even outright cutting their own hair. Please know that I don't judge, as I have been guilty of this myself.

I will say this, though — it doesn't make any difference whether or not you have a cosmetology license, as it's rare to get consistently high-quality cuts when you perform them yourself. Some men have cut their own hair with clippers without a problem. They may not need anything more than a shorter length with a simple shape, so it works for them. We have to determine what works for us. As long as people are happy, I am fine with it. I don't worry about running out of heads of hair to cut in the salon.

As long as you feel good about your hair the majority of the time, there's no harm in giving it a snip here and there, as long as you're not compromising the structure of the haircut and your service at the salon. However, if solo snipping is a constant occurrence, and you don't feel good about your hair on most occasions, then there is a bigger issue to look at. I feel that we all have to be realistic about time, money, schedules and priorities. Some hairdressers may not agree with this view, but my opinion is that we accommodate the client's needs above all else.

Chapter 7

Which Colored Jewels Look Best on a Crown?

Now that we've examined the complexities of haircuts, let's move on to hair color. Hair color can raise just as many questions as haircuts, as perceptions are an inevitable factor here too. Finding the perfect fit for someone's taste, lifestyle, budget and time commitment goes hand in hand with the right selection of color.

A person's choice of hair color can say as much about her personality as her haircut and style. Hair is a symbol of adornment, much like the princess's crown, and the color of our hair represents the jewels on that crown. The investment of jewels can say a lot about the crown and kingdom of a princess. Even if only one jewel is missing from the setting, or if the jewels are mismatched, the perception and value of the crown can change completely. And so it is with hair color.

As with jewels, certain hair colors may appear fake and gauche to some, while other types of color may be too subtle for others to even notice. People have often looked to hair color to help shape their identity — for example, consider Lucille Ball and Marilyn Monroe. In similar cases, hair color is extremely valuable to a woman's persona and her public image. Even if there is no fame involved, it's still a signature for many. Some prefer their hair color and crowns to be more like tiaras, which are more delicate, and offer a subtler statement. This can translate into the world of color as a simple expression of enhanced gloss or shine.

Why Is There So Much Confusion?

Confusion occurs with hair color for many reasons. The main reason is that color looks different depending on the lighting. In essence, it is determined by the refraction of light, which is the bending of light as it passes through one transparent substance and into another. This is why color looks brighter in the sun, and reveals much brighter tones than it does when we are inside shopping at the grocery store, or in front of our bathroom mirror. The color on the head is the same; the way it appears in the light is always different. Oftentimes, clients have left my salon and gone home to their bathroom, only to see something completely different. Some clients are understandably alarmed by this, and will call the salon to schedule a review. The review, given the salon lighting, is puzzling for them, as they recognize that their color is no different than it was the day they left the salon, even though that very same morning it appeared too dark or brassy gold.

Refraction of light is only one aspect to consider when it comes to hair color. Many see different things in refracted light. Have you ever argued over whether a dress was dark blue or black? Or noticed how red cars sometimes appear brown at night?

How many people do you know who are color blind? Why do some people prefer peach over pink?

It's all related to the perceived color registered by the brain. Finding the correct hair color that suits a person in all lighting can be tricky, especially when people offer opinions on the matter. Comments can affect how someone feels about it, and their confidence in wearing it. It's all a matter of preference. It's like apples and oranges, or the way we drink our coffee. There is no right or wrong, just different tastes.

Vicky's True Color

Vicky was a client of mine who stopped coming in a few years ago, after a color concern. At first, she had been referred to me and was excited to see what new ideas I would have for her. Then, after a thorough consultation, we decided that the dark color she had come in with was too drab for her. We decided that a subtle change with warmer tones and a sparkle of highlights would be an appropriate adjustment for this attractive, mature lady in her late sixties.

She loved her new look, and I enjoyed watching her confidence build as she prepared to step back into her world, smiling at her reflection while making her way over to the reception to check out. Within a week, however, she called and asked to come back in. She said that she loved it, and that her husband liked it too, but that she had had lunch with her friends, and someone had asked her why she had so much red in her hair, and remarked that they didn't like it.

This so-called friend told her she felt obligated to tell her because she assumed no one else would, but that they were all thinking the same thing. Her friend said she had a moral obligation to be honest.

I'd like to believe that Vicky's friend had good intentions. However, Vicky was so affected by the comment that she booked an appointment and came in to have her hair restored to her original color. I never saw her again after that, and it made me feel sad. The loss of the client was one thing, but I was even more saddened to see the another person's words have such a negative effect on her. Maybe Vicky sensed my disappointment, and that's why she never came back. Perhaps she felt judgment from my end. I could be wrong about that too. In the end, it's all about perception and where we feel comfortable. It is not for me to decide which color will make Vicky feel her best. It is my job to recommend options, but the choice is ultimately hers. I truly want her to be happy with whatever color she sees.

Why is Salon Color So Expensive?

This is a question that many people struggle with. Here are just a few of the reasons why salon color can be pricey:

1. The time involved.

2. The training required to develop expertise.

3. The setting in which the color service is provided.

4. The cost of the color itself.

The cost of the color product is not as pertinent as the first two things listed. The salon facilitation, the training and time involved to develop the expertise is where the investment is made. The expensive weekends and time spent in training classes, without pay, to improve one's skills is a consideration for salon costs. This is in order to develop the knowledge required to deliver the best results to clients. An attorney does not necessarily charge for the paper he uses to file a lawsuit, even though there is a cost to consider with the paper. Rather, he charges primarily for the time involved in filing the court documents accurately, and for the intellectual property he acquired in his education. The attorney is paid not because he has the paper, but because he knows what to write *on* the paper. Not all attorneys are qualified equally, and some specialize in different fields; the same goes for doctors. There are mainstream skills that any professional should have in order to practice his profession, yet not all charge according to their level of skill. Hairstylists are no different. Make sure to do your research, as you would any other professional service, before you proceed.

Is It Better to Venture Outside the Castle for Color?

People wear costume jewelry as a clever decoy to avoid paying for the authentic jewels, and to protect themselves against the risk of loss, theft or damage. Hair color is very much the same. Many clients have paid outrageous prices for counterfeit high-quality color services, and have suffered huge losses both financially and emotionally. It only adds insult to injury when a high ticket is presented after low-quality work. Consequently, many have chosen to resort to other means, with respect to their time and budget, even if it means limiting their options.

Over the counter color is an option that works well for some and proves disastrous for others. Those who are pleased with this option experience an understandable sense of control and empowerment. They have no desire to venture into the costly and unfamiliar territory of salon color. I have met clients who have done an excellent job of maintaining their color, and some have even delighted in recruiting their husbands to help with the application.

I understand why this is the best option for them, and so I would never discredit these resourceful men and women. I will mention that my most loyal client was once an at-home color applicator. She and her husband worked wonderfully together. She was able to create a predictable color at minimal cost over a glass of wine with her prince. So, why did she need a Hairy Godmother?

Unfortunately, there were no servants to clean up the mess afterward, or to style her royal highness' tresses with a beautiful blowout. She wanted to have the full royalty experience, at her time of choosing, and without having to request permission from his majesty. She saw the value of service, and can now have any jewel she wants, and enjoy the process of trying it on. The Queen of England would never be caught wearing costume jewels because she is well aware of the importance and value of crown jewels. They are guarded carefully and considered priceless. The guards at the Tower of

London keep a watchful eye over the Queen, and so the Queen trusts them. It should be the same with your Hairy Godmother, and with your color, or your precious crown jewels!

How Long Should Color Last?

There is no definitive answer to this question, as there are so many factors involved: rate of growth, lifestyle, frequency of shampoos and hair porosity. The chemicals used in the coloring process, as well as the choice of shade, are all considerations to be made.

1. Rate of growth: Some clients have faster-growing hair than others, and even though that is a major factor regarding the need for maintenance, another thing to consider is how drastic the chemically-enhanced color is from the natural hair color growing in? Also, what is the placement of the heavily contrasting hair color, and how many contrasting colors are in the hair? More modern techniques have blended natural looks with enhanced coloring, which minimizes maintenance at the roots.

2. Lifestyle: Different activities can affect the longevity of color. Swimming in chlorine pools, and saltwater too, will affect hair color. Red and darker hair colors fade much faster — or at least more noticeably. Bleach blondes have to be cautious of chlorine buildup, which reveals itself in a greenish tint if they spend a lot of time in the pool

or Jacuzzi. This is especially true if these women have very porous hair.

3. Frequent Shampoos: It is widely known that hair color fades faster the more it is shampooed. Some shampoos are harder than others, and water temperature also affects the rate at which the color fades. The hotter the water during daily shampoos, the more the cuticle opens and releases color particles.

4. Chemical Process to Achieve Color: There are many different types of color that use a variety of chemical approaches and solutions to deliver color to the hair. The length of time the color lasts depends on the strength of these chemicals and their different objectives.

Some choose color based on activity and style, while most consider the value of investment in time and money. Most clients schedule a retouch base color every four to six weeks, depending on rate of growth and their daily activities. Male clients get color every three weeks or less, as there is much more of a stigma for men who reveal their gray roots. Men would rather come to the salon more frequently than risk facing criticizing eyes. Blonde highlights can go up to three months between appointments, depending on their placement and the amount received and how they are placed. Heavily placed highlights on dark hair may only get six weeks.

The current trends of ombre and bayalage techniques offer much more mileage when it comes to special effects contrasting color. The softer blends of color are optimal with more natural looks in the transition of color from the scalp, and offer minimal maintenance options. The decision is personalized, and your Hairy Godmother must guide her princess to make the best decision that caters to her specific needs. This is sometimes a difficult and daunting task for both the princess and the Hairy Godmother, as both parties must communicate effectively to reach the best decision. Once again, a thorough consultation will target the princess' needs and help put her on the right track.

Our Approach to Color Consultations

When someone comes into our salon for color, we approach the matter in a similar way we do haircuts. We simplify the process by breaking hair color down into three categories:

1. **Light and Dark**: How light or dark would you like your hair to be?

2. **Desired Tone:** Do you prefer warm, neutral or cool tones?

3. **Placement — How Much and Where?** Decide between a single color or a multidimensional with a bold option, or select a more subtle contrast.

We work with our clients using pictures, to identify what they are really asking for by organizing their needs in this manner. Once they know how light or dark they want their hair in relation to the color they have, they can decide whether they want enhanced warmer tones or cooler tones. We can then focus on the multi dimensions and the types of contrasts by discussing how the color will be placed. We use pictures to help illustrate the different shades as well as explain placement.

These basic categories condense the decision making process. Only a few pictures are needed, as they are closer to her target, streamlining the process and reducing confusion. These pictures help us determine her *specific* goal early on in the consultation. We focus on just two or three images so that we can confirm we understand what they are asking for. While this simplifies the process of discovering what a client wants, there is still much to consider regarding the application and delivery.

My fellow hairdressers understand that we have to consider the realities and implications of the client's best interests by learning more about her goals and priorities, both in the salon chair and in her everyday life. Time and budget, as well as the texture of hair, have to be considered too.

It is so helpful when our clients come prepared with an understanding of their priorities. Here are some questions to consider before your next appointment.

1. What has or hasn't worked in the past?
   Focus on the things you want, and that
   have worked for you, when you go in for
   your consultation.

2. Have you identified your highest priority?

   Is it Queen for a day, with high maintenance
   color that requires more frequent visits to
   the salon?

Or would you rather be a lady in waiting,
with longevity and less maintenance?

Once you recognize your highest priority, your Hairy
Godmother can provide you with your best options.
Princesses often get into trouble when they self-diagnose
and issue instructions for specific techniques and
how-tos, rather than focus on their desired end result.
As long as her royal highness is realistic about what she
wants to see in the mirror at the end of the appointment,
her Hairy Godmother should be able to take her on the
least arduous journey.

The Language of Color

The language of color can be confusing, no matter
which side of the chair we are on. Hairstylists have
terms like *double process*, *bayalage*, *ombre* and
color balancing, which are all specific techniques.
Hairstylists have terms that are frequently used, and that
are understood within the industry, as well those that are
used exclusively in their own salon environments. How
is a client supposed to understand what to ask for? Well,
asking for a specific technique often leads to surprising
results. It is always better to focus on the desired end
result in the consultation with a picture, rather than to
try to assess the technique or delivery system.

Clients come to us with their own language too. I've
come across some hilarious descriptions of color. Here
are a couple of my favorites:

Low Beams: Requested by my client from Brazil, who struggled with her English — she meant she wanted *lowlights*.

Buttered Toast: Jean is a lovely lady who, while looking at her toast one morning, had an epiphany and identified a way to describe her base color and highlight tone to us. Each time she leaves with a new color, we smile and say *Buttered Toast!*

The Blonde Rainbow: Red, Brass, Yellow, Orange, Gold, Ash, Gray, White

Blondes are in a category all of their own. I have seen more problems with blondes than any other color category. Other hair dressers share similar accounts of a client's perception of "brassy" as opposed to "buttery gold." Experience has minimized my problems in the salon with this, now that I understand how to get a client's bearing on what they perceive as red, brass or yellow; and orange versus gold. Consultations with blondes are focused on tone, and on the client's perception of tone and placement. We will look at several pictures of various tones, and will ask the client to identify what they think looks brassy. I assess what looks neutral and what looks cool to them. Often, what they are pointing at does not reflect my interpretation of red or orange. I believe the descriptive words get in the way, and so I always refer to pictures for accurate and predictable results. I learned a valuable lesson about this ten years ago, while working at another salon.

Elise's Tale

Elise was a client who was frustrated with her blonde hair. She had lots of light blonde highlights. It almost looked like an allover double-processed blonde. When I first saw her, I felt that she needed lowlights. However, after consulting with her, it was clear that she was adamant that she wanted the yellow out of her hair; she believed it looked brassy and needed more lift. Elise was naturally a dark blonde, and so it was easier to make a bright platinum blonde from that base. I put more highlights in her hair, and brought her to the lightest blond possible without melting her hair off.

Incredibly, Elise said her hair still looked yellow, yet to me it appeared almost white. It was getting a little tense, but she rebooked the appointment for another one in five weeks. When she came in, she complained that she had hated it from start to finish. She felt brassy and yellow.

I explained that I just couldn't make it any lighter, as there had already been so many foils on her head. I felt that the only alternative was to consider allover bleach. Finally, I picked up a hair magazine and flipped through the pages, trying to find something that would help. And as it turned out, Reese Witherspoon was on the cover of the magazine, and Elise spotted it and screamed, "See? That's what I want!"

To my amazement, the color was a heavily contrasted pale blonde with lots of darker lowlights. After talking to Elise, I realized that she needed the contrast of the cool toned lowlights to make the blonde look less yellow. I hadn't gone with my gut at the beginning because I'd thought Elise had wanted to be lighter. I had ruled out lowlights as an option altogether because I'd been afraid that she would feel they were too dark. The lesson I learned that day has been invaluable to me. Pictures are absolutely essential in my consultations, especially with blondes — that way they can be more fun!

A Graceful Way to Gray

Why does gray look good on some and not on others? How can we tell when it's time to grow it out?

These are questions I am asked often. I notice that people who let their roots grow out at the grocery store, or around town. I want to tell them that they have other options, but I don't know how to approach them without offending them, or without them feeling suspicion that I am just trying to hustle some business. I want to tell them that they can talk to their hairstylist about other chemical options while they're in transition. The transition can be fun, with a lighter color change or highlights.

I believe that a person knows when they are ready to make that kind of decision, and that it is my job to make the transition as smooth as possible. Sometimes it can take a year, and sometimes it can take as little as six months. It really depends on how long the hair is, and how much color there is at the beginning. When asked to give my opinion, I have obliged. I gave an opinion a couple of years ago, though, and I was totally wrong.

Diane's Venture Into Gray

Diane is in her seventies, and I had been coloring her hair four years. She liked her hair short, and in a conservative natural blonde shade. Diane would book for highlights every other appointment. One day, however, she said was thinking about growing out her gray, and asked for my opinion

I wasn't convinced it was such a good idea because I thought it may make her look older. I discouraged her from going gray.

Diane mentioned that she was going to be home a lot due to an upcoming surgery, and so hair color would be one less thing to worry about. It made sense that this would be the best opportunity to give the gray a try. I explained the process and said it may take about six months, and that it would involve lightening her current color to diffuse the new growth. Then, we would use demi-permanent colors to help blend the gray through the process. I told her that she would probably end up coloring it again, but that despite my skepticism I supported her decision. We highlighted Diane's hair more heavily at first, and then we switched to demi-permanent colors in lighter shades to help blend the gray while it grew in.

We cut the hair much shorter, and by the fourth month we were well on our way. It did indeed take six months, and at that point I cut her hair in a sassy short style similar to Judy Dench. I recommended that she wear deeper shades of lipstick and slightly bigger earrings, and to lose her pastel clothing for deeper blues and jewel tones. The difference was amazing! Her blue eyes sparkled with her new color combinations.

She looked more vibrant, and dare I say, younger. She sure proved me wrong! I learned that my personal experience does not trump what my client feels is best for her. Diane was tired of coloring her hair and waited until her surgery to make the decision. That was her highest priority.

When presented with a client's decision to grow out their gray, I make recommendations to upgrade jewelry and clothing, and eyeglasses, when transitioning into a modern gray look. I have one client who has exchanged her hair color budget for lash extensions. She looks amazing too! I think this truly is the graceful way to go gray.

Your True Color

Whatever you decide your true color is, that color will shine from within. Trust yourself over other people's opinions. If you feel good in your color, who cares about what other people think? It's your personal choice to make. Consider your options and then trust your decision, and your real Hairy Godmother will support you no matter what!

Chapter 8

Charming Prince Charming

When it comes to charming our salon kings and princes, hairdressers have to be mindful of how to approach his Royal Highness. These masculine majesties have very different needs than their princesses. True love's kiss, in the salon, is found in the acronym K.I.S.S. (Keep It Simple, Sweetheart). For the most part, I find that men don't have the time for in-depth discussions about their hair. Brief bullet-pointed agendas are much more appreciated and far more effective for the male client. Keeping the consultation short and executing the haircut accurately is more of a priority for men.

In my experience, men seem to be much more task-oriented in the salon, than they are experience-driven. That being said, the Hairy Godmother should be a truly welcoming and friendly service provider for male clients. Gentlemen appreciate a convenient, economical and time-efficient appointment that's hassle free. For the most part, men are happiest when they don't have to deal with too much while in the salon chair. Men generally don't express the same excitement that women do when they arrive for their appointment; they are more delighted when there is no wait, as long wait times are often deal-breakers for men, when faced with a chronically late hairdresser. After years of reforming, I now pride myself on being punctual for appointments.

Men seem to enjoy their time in my salon, as long as they are not kept there for too long.

Men, like women, have evolved from their traditional roles. It's not just the urban and metro males expressing particularities at the salon. Men's grooming is one of the fastest growing markets in the salon industry right now, and I'm pleased to say that men have many more choices with new male signature brands and standalone products. The rapid growth of men's grooming and booming trends have shown that the modern man enjoys a hybrid of efficiency and an enhanced salon experience. It's not just men's haircare products that are booming; skin products for the face and body are much more popular than in the days of old. The *metrosexual* stigmas are becoming a thing of the past as men embrace their right to higher-end, professional grooming services.

Although men may not often seek out a personal relationship with their hairstylist, I have found them to be very loyal once that salon relationship has been established. It has been my experience that different genres seem to have different views of what an acceptable haircut is. I often hear men say that "the difference between a good haircut and a bad haircut is about two weeks," which is indicative of their casual approach to men's hair care. I have found that modern men enjoy a shampoo and massage, opting for a more enhanced and pampering experience in the salon than many of the older baby-boomer male clients.

Over the years, I have had to coax older gentlemen to enjoy shampoos that they considered nothing more than a frivolous waste of time. These men will tolerate the service more than they'll enjoy it. This is why many men prefer barber shops over salons. Could it be that these guys were socially-programmed to stigmatize the salon industry as the result of the beauty shops of their younger years? Salons in the 50's and 60's were social hubs for women, with standing weekly appointments. The stereotypical pattern of salon gossip was something that few men enjoyed, and that many men avoided altogether.

Although I wasn't around then, I inherited residual parts of this type of clientele and culture in the very early days of my career. It's almost as if there was salon segregation for male and females. Men went to barber shops and women went to beauty parlors. Both men and woman were much more limited in the choices that were socially acceptable for them at the time.

Women in particular were at the mercy of social pressures, perceptions and expectations by members of the community. As a result, I experienced a less forgiving tone from the "roller set brigade" of women from this genre --especially if their expectations weren't met in the salon. The pressures they experienced in those days were present at social clubs, and other community gatherings which often infiltrated the salon, particularly when it came to prime appointment times on Fridays.

Times are changing, though, and these ladies aren't venturing out to salons to claim their weekly spot under the dryer the way they once did. I don't even own those setting rollers anymore. Weekly blow outs are the modern service equivalent, bringing about another generation with different social pressures. The salon is a place to recharge and feel pampered; it is not necessarily the gossip hub of the past. Men are much more comfortable in a salon environment these days. Not all are set in their ways, though, as perceived by many women.

It's no secret that there is banter between the genders, both inside and outside the salon. Comedy shows and sitcoms have been highlighting the differences between the sexes for years. Occasionally, in my salon, we will share funny stories from the female perspective. There is no malice in this, and it is not meant to offend anyone. I appreciate humor and think that sometimes we are too critical of ourselves, and of each other. Laughter is a culture I encourage in my business. Men seem to enjoy the ease and comfort of this environment, and we all laugh together. The barriers and stigmas are softened; and as a result, people tend to be less guarded.

Pam's Tale

Pam is a new client in her forties, and she shared this story a short time ago. She has long blond hair, which looked marvelous at her last appointment, and we told her that her husband was going to love it! She remarked that he probably wouldn't notice and then shared this story:

A couple of years ago, Pam came home after spending four hours at a salon. She had received a new hair color with highlights and low lights, and paired it with new long hair extensions.

Pam arrived home excited about her brand new look, and couldn't wait to show her husband.

She walked in to where he was sitting and did a runway model turn for him, so that he could take in her wonderful new look and celebrate it with her. He smiled as she twirled around in front of him. She smiled back, and then asked, "What do you think?"

He replied with genuine enthusiasm, "Wow! Nice new coat!"

What's worse, the coat wasn't even new.

It's been a popular belief that women dress solely to impress their men. The social pressures from the Mad Men era of the 50's and 60's, however, are becoming extinct with the average contemporary woman. The modern princess dresses for *herself* and values the opinion of the court and her sister princesses, which often outranks a man's appreciative eye.

Some ladies of the court still compete with one another, while other ladies look for simple acceptance. It has become less about the prince and more about social pressures. The focus in today's world is not necessarily how to catch a prince, but how to measure up in one's social and professional circles. Our social evolution in traditional male and female roles has altered the perceptions of the roles depicted in fairytales. Even the Disney stories have adapted to modern times, offering more dynamics and depth in both male and female characters.

Rookies and Kings

I struggled with male clients in the early days of my career. I was a talkative rookie, and not yet proficient in my cutting skills. I dreaded working on men, as I was insecure and easily intimidated. The quiet ones always scared me the most. I knew there was no margin for error because men don't use curling irons and hairsprays. Men can't disguise a bad cut other than with a hat. Each time I escorted a male client to check out, I was hyperaware that my work was on full display.

This fear caused me to cringe each time I gave a man a haircut, struggling to conceal my nerves regarding backlash or criticism. Back then, I relied on intense focus, paired with nervous chatter, while men have sat stonefaced in my salon chair, staring at their reflection in silence. I'd never know what they were thinking, yet their stiff body language screamed at me. It was very scary. It took me several years to get through all that nervousness and I'm so glad those days are over! Not all men were so stone-faced, though. There have been some very funny comments made to me by men. The following story is one that comes to mind.

George's Tale — The Beauty and the Leash

George is a retired attorney from Charleston, South Carolina, and was a client of mine at another salon about ten years ago. He enjoyed the salon environment, although he would spend more time looking in the mirror admiring pretty ladies walking by, than focus on getting his hair cut. At times, it was hard to keep his head from tilting as he gazed past me.

We were in a centrally-located salon, and people would always stop by to say hello to our beloved and beautiful owner, Bev.

One lady in particular used drop by the salon with her Yorkshire terrier. The little dog would appear first, in the mirror's reflection, and almost seemed to drag its owner, who was a very scruffy-haired elderly woman clinging to the leash. Upon noticing this, George raised his eyebrows and leaned in to me. "Well my Staahhhrs," he said, "from here it's really haahhhrd to tell which one's on the end of the leash." He was so bad, but I couldn't help but chuckle at that.

Bonsai and the Barber

Once loyalty has been established and a man is comfortable in his salon castle, he becomes more flexible and forgiving as a client, and will often stay around for years. I have had male clients who have become dear friends, but it usually takes years to build that kind of rapport. Take, for instance, a male client who has been with me for over ten years, whom I affectionately call Bonsai.

The name was given as a sort of call sign to acknowledge the approach I'd have to take for his haircare. Bonsai was originally referred to me by dear my friend, who happened to be his wife, after he had been slightly traumatized by a buzz cut.

Bonsai is a fun, happy-go-lucky chap, in his forties, with an incredible sense of humor. This self-employed painting contractor was always confident and at ease in the salon environment. He'd previously enjoyed a comfortable, long-term relationship with a male hairstylist, who had abruptly left the area following a nasty breakup with his partner.

Bonsai had felt so safe in the salon that he really didn't give too much thought about the next stop. He was oblivious to the dangers that would lurk in one particular barber's chair. Bonsai had been recommended to the barber by his brother, and so Bonsai went willingly, like a sheep to the slaughter. The skilled barber used clippers, and without any kind of consultation, all of Bonsai's perfect hair was on the floor.

It took four months for his hair to grow back. Our first appointment together involved a clear conversation and an understanding that I would "trim" very carefully, as if his hair were a bonsai tree. No more clippers for this guy! His bad experience at the barbershop could have been avoided with a brief conversation. It took me less than five minutes to listen to Bonsai—and now I've retained his business for years!

It's important to understand that men have needs too, and that they just don't express them like women do. Men are supposed to be strong and tough. They are our heroes. They're also human, and many are kind and sensitive. Oftentimes, women give men a bad rap. I, too, have been guilty of this. We all know that we shouldn't judge, yet we do it anyway.

My insecurities and preconceived ideas affected the quality of my service, especially in my early years. I was much more comfortable with women than I was with men. The next story illustrates the transition in my career, and in my personal relationships with male clients. You will notice how barriers and boundaries were poorly managed, as well as how they evolved over time.

The Surprising Saga of Richie Rich

In 1993, I ventured into the world of salon ownership. I was still relatively new to the business, and not yet a confident hairdresser, especially when it came to men's cuts. One day, a man walked into my salon, claiming he had been referred to me by another client. He stood in his *Gold's Gym* muscle shirt, with long curly hair, shaped in to the most glorious mullet I had ever seen.

He was a classic stereotype for Myrtle Beach at the time. He was a beach-bodied male with an eye for the ladies and a chip on his shoulder. He was so handsome and charismatic with his sparkling blue eyes, tanned skin and dazzling white smile, that he could actually pull it off. In fact, the only unattractive thing about him was his attitude. He was cynical and sarcastic toward women, and had clearly become locked and loaded in his male chauvinistic humor.

I knew I didn't want to work with him. I was a married woman with children, and had very conservative views; a strong mind with an even sharper tongue. His arrogance posed a threat for a possible confrontation that would not end well for either of us. I set up an appointment for him with one of my young and very willing stylists, who happened to be far more eager than I was to earn his business.

This man did not go unnoticed in the salon chair, and he often baited me, spinning around playfully in the chair when he could. He was on the cusp of annoying at times, but he stayed in the safety and common language of humor. Through these exchanges, I later learned that a betrayal and bad breakup had jaded this blue-eyed hunk from Dallas, Texas.

Over the next year, I began to read between the lines, and was able to discern his hurt through the humor. I think he saw the sincerity in my beliefs. He recognized that I was an honorable and loyal woman, despite my own hidden insecurities. He landed in *my* salon chair a time or two, and within a year, after the other stylist left, he became a regular client of mine.

I even confessed that I didn't feel comfortable with him at first, which was why he had been deferred. He claimed that he'd picked up on my negative vibe, but decided to stick it out anyway, just to prove a point.

A turning point in our relationship came about over a chance meeting, as he walked by the closed salon and noticed I was alone, redoing the holiday window display. He motioned for me to let him in, so I opened the door. It was New Year's Day, and the conversation flowed comfortably as we exchanged post-holiday accounts of time spent with family. It was during his account that my respect for him grew.

He announced that he had just discovered he was going to be a "daddy." I was stunned that this Casanova character, who was in his mid-twenties, and prime, had taken such life-changing news so well. The responsibility of fatherhood did not seem to match who

I thought he was. After his announcement, he stated that he was going to do the "right thing" and marry the mom-to-be, who had been his girlfriend for the past several months. He said that even though he was not quite ready, he felt that marriage was a pledge to the mother of his child, and a commitment to being a good dad. Who would have guessed that this young man had traditional values? I shared my concern for his dilemma and conveyed my respect for him stepping up and taking responsibility. He was lighthearted about it all, but we both acknowledged the depth of his decision. He bid me farewell for the day, and I felt like the New Year had brought about a new Richie. And I was right—it had.

I watched this man, whom I'd once considered a "punk," transform into the most loyal husband and loving father. I respected him more and more as I watched him exchange his muscle shirt for a business suit and a short haircut, driven by the need to be a strong provider for his family. He struggled through a year of laboring to find his niche in Myrtle Beach. It was a hard leap to make in a resort town, and so he chose to move back to Dallas in search of better opportunities. I was sad to see him go, as I sometimes thought of him as a sort of younger cousin, despite the fact that he often said, "What's up, Mama?" when calling for appointments. He most often used the unique phrase, "Hello you English Conniggett!" Whatever that means.

Life went on, and the salon grew busier. Then, two years later the phone rang and I heard that familiar, yet unique phrase again. "Hello, you English Conniggett! I 'm back!" Amazingly, Richie had moved back to Myrtle Beach for a job opportunity. He arrived with his family in tow, including his wife and two-year-old and a new baby on the way. His wife had wanted to be closer to family, and so Richie had found a job in the area as a sales rep for a local wine distributor. It was great to have him back!

As our lives and marriages matured, we became the greatest of friends. He and I both faced challenges of mental illness with our spouses. My heartache began a few years before his. Richie showed me support in the most unexpected waves of kindness. He was thoughtful in a way that would make any mother proud.

One day in particular comes to mind for me. It had been a long, tough day at the salon, and Richie came in for an after work appointment. I had fought back tears as I cut his hair, trying to make light of things with humor, like we always did. My husband was struggling with bipolar disorder, and had been in and out of a mental hospital, and I carried the burden and blame, from both him and our kids. I had a heavy heart, and was so full of self-doubt. After Richie's haircut, I excused myself, leaving him alone to write his check while I slipped into the backroom to pull myself together. I walked back out to an empty salon and noticed a note taped to my mirror.

It read, *You are an awesome mom.*
You will get through this.

Needless to say, our friendship continued to develop. Richie became as protective of me as any little brother would. I was five years his senior, and so frequently offered big sister advice, as he encountered his own mental illness nightmare with his wife. Our marriages, which were both doomed to fail, contributed to an extraordinary friendship and bond, which has endured for over twenty years now.

We've shared horror stories of trying to co-parent with our bipolar exes. Exchanging bizarre stories was normal for us. I guess it seemed only logical that Richie was the first person to call my salon to warn me of a freak tornado approaching the area on July 6, 2001.

I was totally unaware, and thought it a practical joke of his, until I stepped out into the parking lot. I looked up, with Richie still on the phone, and gasped as I saw a dark cloud swirling across the street, above the trees of the Myrtle Beach State Park. It passed by without harming me, but the experience was surreal.

Many things were surreal with Richie, but not all of them were disasters. Life eventually called us both to live away in separate cities as we followed new paths, but we still kept in touch. One day, in May 2006, I received an e-mail announcing that Richie had a new bride-to-be. Although I had never met Amanda, I had heard so much about her in previous conversations; I felt that she might be the right match for him.

The nuptials would take place on the island of Maui, in Hawaii, the following November. I was invited to go, and as it happened, the heavens and the universe opened its merciful doors, and I was able to accept the invitation. I had just been through another wave of torment, losing both of my parents, and also a near fatal car accident with my nineteen-year-old son. I was forty-two, and I truly needed a break. Within days of the email, I received news of a modest inheritance from my father, which gave me the opportunity to make the trip to Hawaii.

It was a dream vacation from the start. Arriving in Maui was surreal for me. I journeyed with my longtime boyfriend, Kevin, a highly trained architect who always marveled at the exciting perks and opportunities I received as a hairdresser, despite his eight-year college education.

We rented a convertible and soon found ourselves at an amazing resort on the north shore. We went on a biking trip that took us 35 miles down the mountain, after witnessing the most amazing sunrise I'd ever seen at the top of Haleakala, a dormant volcano. Richie included us in all of the family activities and excursions. Kevin and I were the only non-family members there. We joked that years later, Richie's kids would ask who the random people were in the wedding photographs. I'm sure there have been a lot of other weddings and pictures where the same question was raised. You never know where I may pop up!

It's been almost ten years since Maui. Until recently, it had been about eighteen months since I'd spoken to Richie. I picked up the phone the other day to tell him about my book, and informed him that he would be the featured prince charming. Without skipping a beat, he recognized his "Old English Conniggett."

Our kids are grown now, and one of the first things he said was, "We're old, Mama!"

I exclaimed, "I know. I'm a grandma now!"

We laughed as we recalled some of our times together. He and his wife Amanda are still very happily married and plan on returning to Maui next year for their 10th anniversary and wedding party reunion. I was invited to go and would love to attend if life allows. And the saga continues....

Chapter 9

Castle Walls Keep Us Safe and Happy

It's easy to get swept up in the excitement of meeting your Hairy Godmother. You've finally found that special someone who understands your hair needs, and you finally trust that she can cut, color and shape your tresses at the salon, making it easier for you to manage each and every day in your castle. There are no more bad hair days and frustrating style struggles in front of the mirror, and as a result, you look and feel great.

The joyful anticipation of regular visits to the salon castle will only add to the strength of your bond with your Hairy Godmother. You may even think of going the extra mile to show your appreciation, by surprising her with her favorite coffee drink on your next visit, for example. Maybe you'll bring a cookie, or fresh cut flowers from your palace garden. Your Hairy godmother loves all of these things!

Over time, your Hairy Godmother may be blessed with the ultimate privilege of receiving her very own invitation to the ball. She is honored to share in a royal family event, such as the joys of your wedding day or your baby shower.

Most importantly, you'll see that she will also be there for you in dark times too, listening and comforting you during the betrayal of a bitter breakup or divorce. She will share in your heartache as you cope with the loss of a terminally ill parent or loved one, or stand with you in the face of a shocking loss or sudden change. Your Hairy Godmother stays with you through thick and thin, and there is no one like her. You can tell her anything and everything, and sometimes she shares her vulnerabilities and fears too.

There will be times when you want to offer your support and understanding, when your Hairy Godmother is trying to work through her own troubles. A spellbinding friendship grows until you realize you don't know what you would do without her, and that she feels the same way. Sometimes this sweet friendship goes on without a glitch, and then sometimes it's a little more complicated. The roles may get confused, and soon your Hairy Godmother may forget that her main purpose is to help you feel great and look your best in front of the mirror.

Transitional times can bring about distraction, at which point the lines become blurred, and soon she gets so comfortable in your friendship that she is no longer aware of your needs. You find that her ears have stopped listening to the gentle whispers and reminders of what you need while in the salon styling chair. Maybe you've finally reached a point where you're ready to say something stronger to get things back on track, but alas, *her* Mom is sick now, and so you feel it would be too hard on her.

You wait until there is another chance to approach her but it never seems to be the right time. Something always seems to get in the way. Meanwhile, you find yourself waiting patiently for appointments, or leaving shortchanged on service. You feel rushed through and disappointed, yet you still pay the same you've always paid. The service you once could count on has now become a burden that you have to carry. You no longer feel like the special princess or queen she used to honor. How do you get out of this mess? You love your friend but you need her to be your Hairy Godmother. You can always find more friends, but finding a Hairy Godmother isn't so easy. What is a girl to do?

Confession of a Hairy Godmother

I am writing this account because I am a Hairy Godmother who once fell from grace in this way. It has been my honor and pleasure to serve all the people of the kingdom, whether they were princesses or not. It is my goal to help them understand they are as important as any other princess or queen.

It has always been my purpose to help everyone who sat in my chair see the true beauty in their reflection. I want them to learn where the true magic lives; it's in their hearts. These discoveries have often led to close friendships.

Over the years, I've realized that I am a part of something special. I've been blessed with the love and support of dear clients who later became close friends. I adored them so much, and yet I unconsciously slipped into the sea of comfort, not realizing I had come to depend on them to keep me afloat, just as much as they did me. Anyone who reads this and recognizes my guilt — well, I sincerely apologize. I still think of the clients who were so loyal to me, and whom I inadvertently took for granted. I became mystified by our amazing bond, which grew into an affection that shattered the normal realms of conventional friendships. A friendship with your stylist is complicated. It is a friendship born and bound in a service that the princess *needs*. And it is my responsibility to take care of my princess, not the other way around.

Escaping the Chains of Complication

So how do we get out of this mess? It's tricky, isn't it? There are three things a person can do in these kinds of situations:

1. Accept your circumstances

2. Change your circumstances

3. Disconnect from your circumstances

It is not for me to decide which option you choose. I will say I've seen many people confess their misery to me, and still choose to stay in stylist relationships — and other relationships for that matter — for far too long, especially when it is clear that there is no hope. Hidden resentment builds its silent walls, blocking any hope of recovery the longer you wait.

For those who feel stuck, this is a form of acceptance. When people ask me about this dilemma, I recommend disconnecting if the relationship is beyond repair. In this dynamic, even a marriage can fail and counseling may offer the only hope. The good news is that you're not married to your hairstylist, although the obligation to stay by her side can be quite overwhelming. Keep in mind that you are free to leave if the relationship becomes too much. Remember that you are paying for a service. Having said this, I realize for some it's easier said than done.

Few people feel they are able to change their patterns when things have become so entrenched. Invariably, any attempt to change the relationship raises the risk of even more complications, although there is a way to move past this.

A good way to start is to focus on the dynamics of the relationship and how *you* relate to your hairdresser — or to anyone else, for that matter. What messages are *you* sending?

Boundaries can be reset in many relationships, and at any given time. Our response to the situation is a key factor. We can change the way we react to things at any point we choose, by doing the three things listed previously. Clients have caught my attention by reminding me of things in gentle ways. I have been guilty, in my excitement over an upcoming event or an impending doom, to get distracted instead of focusing on my service. I have become more aware of this in recent years, and strive to stay focused. I have heard clients — mine and others' —complain that this is a common problem with other stylists too.

During periods of distraction my clients have been very clever and said, "I can't wait to hear the latest news, but let's talk about my hair first. Do you have a few extra minutes? Because I am struggling."

This is a cue for me to pay attention, and it works! If your friend or stylist is too busy to listen, then meeting for an honest conversation outside the salon is the next best thing. Set a time and place as soon as you decide you need to talk. This is crucial when it comes to reaching a resolution. Let her know that you will need 100% focus and attention during your brief time together, and that it's important to you. Be sure to make it clear that you need to talk about your hairstylist-client relationship, and not a current styling issue. It is alright to show you're hurt, but refrain from expressing your anger or bitter disappointment, in an effort to bring all defenses down.

Have a solution in mind a rather than focusing on the problem. Talk about specifics you need to change and how you want to move forward. Once the dynamics of your relationship have been reset, then it's time to focus on the hair itself.

This sounds like it may be uncomfortable, and it certainly can be at first, but if both parties are open to listening and finding a solution, it can bring about very positive changes. It's like marriage counseling — it can go either way.

If you have a Hairy Godmother who respects you, and if you show the same respect, it's possible that you can remain friends and end the professional relationship. It's like dating — some exes you may still get along with, and others you simply can't. I have friends who used to be clients, and I still enjoy spending time with them, but we've both come to realize that it's better to keep the boundaries simple. I have learned so much from uncomfortable situations, and so I can confirm that there is no comfort in growth and no growth in comfort.

More often, clients will choose to disconnect completely and find a new salon home. This can be painful for the oblivious hairstylist; yet amazingly, it is the silence of her long lost client and friend that will make her more alert for the princess to take a seat in her chair. It's a hard lesson to learn, but I've learned and accepted it.

You have to decide whether it is worth the effort of salvaging the friendship or the service relationship. You may find that things get worse instead of better, and then you are forced to walk away. As painful as it can be, sometimes it is far healthier to leave a salon relationship than to stay in one that is making you feel bad.

The Little Princess, the Queen and the Queen's Mother

Years ago, a beautiful little princess walked into my salon. She was sweet and sparkly-eyed and full of life. She was twenty-one years old, and we had such a lovely time together at the salon that she ran home to her castle to share the wonderful news of her Hairy Godmother. The Princess told the Queen, and soon she and the Queen's mother began scheduling regular appointments. Things seem to go well for several months, but it wasn't long after that trouble amongst the royals began to reveal itself.

The little princess had met a bad prince, and she wanted to leave the castle to be with him. The little princess told me she had found a job making great money "dancing." She knew that if the Queen and the Queen's mother knew, then there would be big trouble, and so I was sworn to secrecy. Now, the Queen and the Queen's mother knew that something wasn't right. They would torture me with heartbreaking accounts of how worried they were about the little princess. I too was worried about the young girl. It was very hard to stay objective in this situation.

The little princess stopped coming as often, and eventually she started missing appointments. I tried to convince her to talk to her family, but she refused until she stopped coming in altogether. The Queen and the Queen's mother had become more and more difficult, and I felt so bad for them that I revealed what I knew. Needless to say, the whole thing blew up in my face and no one lived happily ever after. I came to work one morning to discover that a brick had been thrown through my salon window. I will never know how that story ended. I do know, however, that I learned a lot about boundaries that day.

Boundaries Are the Walls That Keep Us Safe

We often hear the word *boundaries* and the need for them, but what does that look like in the salon environment? I find it easy to connect to people because I am such an open book, and I enjoy sharing my feelings and experiences with others. I love to hear my clients' stories about their travels, and their different professions and family lives. I see a common link in people from all walks of life, and from different countries too. The variation fascinates me, as we all share the same basic elements of human emotion: the fear of loss and the need for connection.

Time and trust will always bring a connection closer, both inside and outside of the salon. The relationships I've developed at the salon have to be managed appropriately in order to prioritize the integrity of the service. I have found that maintaining a clear understanding with my clients from the very beginning is essential. This helps things stay where they are supposed to be.

I will gently remind clients that every time they walk through my salon door, we are to focus on their hair and the consultation first, and then to catch up with the latest news once we've covered everything else. I remind them that it is *their* opportunity to speak, just as they did when I met them at their first appointment. I reiterate that I am their hairdresser first and foremost.

My fiduciary responsibility is to their service while at the salon. We can schedule social time, but at the salon I am their hairdresser. This also sets the tone for "drop-in visits," as clients realize I am working. Keep a safe distance and learn about the person you are with, and remember that salon relationships were initiated out of a need for hair services.

Your hairstylist is your hairstylist above all else. You can have a friend who is a doctor, or an attorney or a mechanic, but when you are in their office or workplace, you want them to be a professional, and they need you to behave like a client. Remember where you are if you have a dual role in someone's life, as it's best not to cross the lines on either side. I have a cell phone for my business, and also a personal cell phone. My friends have both numbers. It is understood that if they have a salon need or question, they call the salon line. This way, when my staff or I pick up the salon line, whether I'm in or have stepped out of the salon, I know they are contacting me because they need their hairstylist, and so I answer the phone in that role, accordingly.

We must always be mindful of others' time, both in our professional or personal relationships. Similarly, we must be reminded that when we have booked and paid for an appointment, it is our time to indulge and enjoy ourselves.

People generally know better than to drop by their attorney's or doctor's office without an appointment. An appointed time is scheduled so that the client can receive the full benefit of the service, and so that the professional is equipped to offer the best service possible. Unfortunately, hairdressers are not always shown the same respect. My clients, however, treat me with the utmost respect, and I believe this is because they understand the level of service I am trying to provide through the boundaries I have set.

Hairstylists have to find a way to offer the best professional service possible, and to navigate the close emotional ties they have with many different people and personalities. It's a wonderful experience, and yet it can be overwhelming at the same time.

I know of bartenders, pharmacists, storekeepers, and sometimes even bank employees who play the roles of both friend and service provider. Some professional fields offer training on how to set and maintain those boundaries. Counselors, and others in the medical and legal fields, are given guidance in terms of where the specific lines are and how they should be managed. Often, hairdressers are not given the emotional guidance they need to protect themselves from the emotional strains of the job. We set up our own coping mechanism attempting to avoid either becoming more overwhelmed or more disconnected from our clients. Coping, in a sense, has replaced self-care. I think we should aim higher, and try to do more than just cope with difficult situations. I learned this from someone who once saw me in a desperate way.

Ending the Reign of Princess Dark Cloud

Ten years ago, not too long after my mother passed away, I was faced with a series of losses. I became overwhelmed, and acted like a victim who'd been tossed around in the harsh winds of life.

One day, I was having an argument with a lifelong friend who was visiting, and who was trying to coach me, yet giving me a hard time. I broke down and sobbed helplessly as I said, "I am coping the best that I can."

In that moment, I heard the words that changed my life:

"I should think that someone like you is capable of far more than just coping."

I glared at my friend through my tears, shocked by the harsh words he'd spoken. I was feeling so vulnerable, but after a long stare, I realized he was right.

I could either take control of my circumstances or let them take control of me. It has been a long journey of setting and re-enforcing boundaries, but it has truly saved me.

A Hairy Godmother's Promise

The princess is not responsible for me. I can be her friend, but I must always be her Hairy Godmother above all else. I will protect the princess by setting safe boundaries and leaving the doors of communication open so that she can ask for anything she needs from me. I will fulfill the role of Hairy Godmother whenever she finds herself within the sacred walls of the salon castle. It is my promise to keep everything she tells me in confidence. And I, in turn, must be strong enough to express when the line between friendship and service is being crossed at the salon. I will do my very best to keep the integrity of the service she deserves, and guard the relationship with boundaries so that the magic is never threatened.

Chapter 10

Bad Spells and Hocus Pocus

What happens after an evil witch has cast an ugly hair spell on you? Where does a princess go for help? Remember the little mermaid and how she was tricked? How can you distinguish a true Hairy Godmother from an evil witch with bad spells and hocus pocus? The horrible truth is that spells in the salon can go terribly wrong, and there isn't always an evil witch that is behind them. It is inevitable that nasty surprises will appear in many other areas of life as well.

Someone may get sick, or lose a job, or get in a car accident. Bad things happen without warning. In life, at any given point, someone is either experiencing a big life change, in the middle of one, or recovering from one. You and your Hairy Godmother are no exception.

The challenge of trying to hold down a job, while staying focus at work, is very difficult during these times of transition. Things tend to carry over from our personal lives to our professional ones, and we may find our attention drifting toward problems that have nothing to do with work. These distractions can cause problems in the workplace, compromising the quality of our performance. It is not always a loss or a tragedy at fault. A wedding, birth of a child, or a move in to a brand new home are equally as distracting.

In a perfect world, we should always be fully focused on the job, and for the most part we probably are. However, there are times when we let things slip, and it seriously affects the people who count on us. We only have to look at our highways to understand the devastation caused by a distracted driver. Similarly, a distracted stylist standing behind the chair can cause emotional harm that may last for months, or even years. The level of severity varies depending on the circumstances. It is important to note, that there is a huge difference in getting a *disappointing* result at a salon as compared to suffering a salon hair trauma.

It is like is buying a car with constant mechanical problems, and then perpetually searching for someone to repair it, rather than being hit in a head-on collision and being in traction for six months, or potentially losing a limb. Hair trauma can be so emotionally upsetting that it can affect people in the long-term, especially when they are faced with a return visit to the salon chair.

Hair trauma doesn't always begin in the salon, though. A childhood memory of being bullied or teased in school because of an irregular hair texture, cut or color can leave deep emotional scars. Some have faced alopecia, or alepcia areata (balding or balding areas) as a result of a disorder or medcial treatments such as chemo.

In these cases, preexisting anxiety or post-trauma often transfer to the salon environment. The trauma is seeded in the fear of being an outcast. Obsessive concern over the hair may serve as a coping mechanism for clients to feel a sense of control. I have witnessed hair anxiety in clients, and have come to learn that it is a complex issue, and a symptom of coping with a deeper trauma that isn't necessarily related to the hair.

A beautiful head of hair can make someone feel more secure about themselves while compensating for other features they may not like as much, or causes feelings of shame. Hair may serve as a veil for a person with acne, or as a distraction from a crooked smile; it may even hide a facial scar. Just look at young girls in their teens these days, and observe the prominence of long hair trends. Hair has the power to make a woman feel good when she is struggling with her age, or her weight, or anything else. A good haircut and style can help her feel more attractive and acceptable.

Not having enough hair, often as a result of hair loss, is also very distressing. Thinning hair is in a category all of its own, especially, when it comes to trauma. The emotional implications are horrible for both men and women, especially when it comes to hiding hair loss from others. Male pattern balding seems to be more widely accepted, and more regularly recognized as a common occurrence; but this can still be just as distressing for men as it is for women. Women have to come to terms with balding in different ways than men, and for different reasons. Menopause and hormonal changes are often a factor, both of which can intensify and complicate things emotionally. The primary cause of the more common types of balding is hereditary The American Academy of Dermatology has more information on hair loss on their website. Dermatologists can address the various treatments and causes.

Women often lean on cosmetic options such as hairsprays and teasing techniques to disguise balding areas in their style, but they are encouraged to exercise caution here, as this may exacerbate the problem. Brushing the hair too harshly with strong-hold hairsprays and continual rough styling will snag fragile hairs, creating a bigger problem than it is solving.

It is best to shampoo and rinse out strong-hold hairsprays rather than brush them out. Extra hold hairsprays should be used as a finishing spray rather than as working sprays. I tend to use a working spray for control while styling, and then a holding spray to finish. I mostly use extra hold sprays as a top coat on a completed style.

Special shampoos promise results that can help, but the results may vary, and they are quite often expensive. Wigs are another option, but they tend to be hot and uncomfortable, although there are has been much improvement over the years, with higher quality wigs that look stunning and are much more comfortable.

I see wonderful and beautiful women in my salon with thinning hair on a regular basis. Sadly, they often lose the joy of the salon experience, as it is replaced with the burden of trying to keep their hair. They are willing to invest in an array of expensive products, and still many of these women feel like they don't get the results they need. These ladies are incredible, and they manage to address their problems in very creative ways.

Alice's Magic Fairy Dust

Alice is in her sixties, and has lovely fluffy white hair which started thinning quite dramatically at the top of her head several years ago. She has a history with thyroid issues, and I believe there are hormonal and stress factors involved, too. Alice has striking features with amber colored eyes, framed beautifully with naturally dark eyebrows, and flawless makeup. Her deep lipstick accentuates her white smile, and she has excellent taste in jewelry, particularly silver. She is very attractive, and her thinning hair is actually the last thing you would notice about her.

However, Alice's hair troubles her greatly, and I wonder if she is even aware of how pretty she is. She has exhausted every effort to resolve the issue, and is now focusing on learning to accept it, and work with what she's got. This lady really tickles me with her creativity when it comes to disguising her balding crown. I want to share a great tip that she taught me.

Alice's hair is so white that it can easily reveal her pink scalp. When she visits the salon, she brings a Wonderbag of her balding hair hacks. My favorite is the tub of cornstarch that she pulled straight from the grocery store shelf, and paired with a makeup brush.

After her blow dry, I simply dip the makeup brush into the tub, tap gently and begin to dust the cornstarch lightly onto Alice's scalp, as if it were makeup powder. The white powder is fine, light and easy on her hair. It disguises her scalp beautifully, without hindering the hairstyling process. Best of all, it costs next to nothing. Brilliant! I think Alice and balding princesses like her are really the queens of resourcefulness in the salon castle.

Hair has the power to empower. Some clients select a style with the primary objective of setting themselves apart in social settings. The idea is to showcase a signature feature to which a high level of emotional importance is attached, establishing a crucial priority in the salon service. This style priority is more than just a look; it becomes a part of the client, and of how she sees herself. It is her message to the world!

In a sense, hair is an expression of the vulnerability of inner beauty, and of our sense of self-acceptance. It is often measured and judged by the outside world, which reflects the value of image we uphold in our inner world.

In a nutshell, for a majority of the western world, hair often serves as the clothing for the most vulnerable, naked parts of our self-esteem. This is why hair trauma is so detrimental.

I have heard hundreds of accounts from hair trauma victims, and I've witnessed its effects. People may say, "It's just hair," but I think not. My experience has taught me to respect the power of hair. I work hard with others to help them heal from the emotional repercussions of hair trauma, as I myself have experienced trauma on both sides of the salon chair. For me, I think seeing how it affects someone else is worse than experiencing it firsthand.

I have had terrible experiences with my own hair, many of which occurred before I became a hairdresser. Hair trauma can truly be a life-changing experience. I would like to share one such account with you that happened to me a long time ago.

Hair Trauma and the Birth of a Hairy Godmother

In 1986, I was twenty-two years old and expecting my first child. I was big and pregnant and feeling very fat. Furthermore, I was always low on cash and time. I was working as a deli manager in a convenience store for a low hourly wage. In those days, when I needed my hair done, it never occurred to me to schedule an appointment in advance. I would ignore my hair needs until I was baited by an ugly reflection in my bathroom mirror, by which point the issue required immediate attention. I appealed to my sparsely funded bank account and settled on the first affordable salon.

I permed my hair in those days, as this was the big trend at the time. I had the day off from work, and so I found a salon where I could walk in without an appointment. I was slightly familiar with the perm process, and knew that it would take a couple of hours, so I was glad to secure an appointment on the spot. The girl didn't seem too friendly at the desk, but that didn't matter much to me. I was focused on the cost and the convenience of the service. After a price check for my medium-length hair, I agreed to the service and my name was jotted down on the appointment book.

The receptionist called over to a young stylist who walked over to me, without smiling, and then led me back to the shampoo bowl. I noticed that, like the receptionist, she didn't seem to have much personality either. I still wasn't worried as I understood that I was getting what I paid for, which was fast efficient service with no frills. I just needed a perm at a good price. I didn't pay attention to processing times. Not my job, right? I didn't think to ask about the risks of perming bleached blonde hair. I'd never had any issues with salon perms in the past. And besides, I had been a box blonde for years.

There was no real consultation; I just told the girl that I wanted a perm that would last as long as possible, and that I didn't mind it being extra curly at first, as I imagined that my hair would loosen after the first few weeks. She nodded her head and got started.

She didn't seem to engage with me as a client, but she did what she was expected to do — right? Besides, I didn't have to worry if she knew what she doing, since she was the professional — right? Wrong!

As far as I can tell, and knowing what I know now, my perm was severely over-processed that day. Plus, the neutralizer was left on for twenty minutes, while my stylist went off to smoke a cigarette. This was back in the 80's, when you could still smoke in a salon. Can you imagine that? I remember that part specifically, as I had to go ask someone to find my stylist. I'd suspected that she might have forgotten about me, as the processing felt much longer than usual. The girl finally returned, with no apology, and began rinsing my hair. I felt rods coming out around my neckline and heard the clinking in the sink, not realizing that in some parts — particularly in the back and around hairline—my hair was still attached to the rod as it fell into the sink. I just assumed that *she* had removed them. After she had taken out the remaining perm rods, she rinsed my head in warm water and conditioned my hair.

She combed through my hair with a pick and walked me over to a hood dryer. I noticed in the mirror that it looked extremely curly when it was wet, and that it got much frizzier after it dried.

I had expected it to look quite curly, but not *that* curly. I was even prepared for a little frizz on some of the ends, which was not uncommon for me until after the cut.

When I was brought back to the salon chair, I took a closer look in the mirror and knew immediately that I didn't like it. My hair was extremely frizzy, plus some of the ends were a little bent and straight-looking. I looked like a blonde head of cauliflower. It was absolutely terrible, but I decided not to panic.

I told myself that it would look better once I got home and fixed it, even though I understood the customary two-day waiting period for shampooing, which was required for new perms. I held on to the hope that it would look better when *I* styled my hair and curled it. But when I stood in front of my bathroom mirror, I realized how badly damaged my hair was.

Have you ever arrived home and discovered the hidden truth about the damage your hairdresser has done? It is one of the most violating things you can feel. It's one thing to look at yourself in the mirror and see the mess staring back at you, but it's an entirely different ordeal to go out in public — or even worse, to have your spouse say something.

My husband didn't see me that night before going to bed. I usually went to bed early, as I had to leave for work at 5 a.m.

He had returned home late that night, and had passed out on the couch, as he often did. Early the next morning, when I leaned in to kiss him goodbye, he was bolted awake from his slumber and said, "Damn baby, what the hell did you do to your hair?" I was horrified and cried all the way to work.

I was a big, fuzzy mess, with gaps throughout my hair from where some of it had broken off. I could feel tram line ridges on my scalp, where the footprints of the perm rods had left their mark. I was big and pregnant and looked a mess. In fact, I'd looked better before I went into the salon. And what about the money I'd paid? It was money I really didn't have to spend. How could someone be so careless? I thought to myself, *I would never do this to anyone.*

That was almost thirty years ago, and I still remember it vividly. Before I became a hairdresser, I was a client who had terrible experiences in the salon chair. That bad perm was the worst, but definitely not the last one I had. However, I was so much more guarded and cautious after that, and forever changed as a client. It was a sharp reminder of why I needed to become a hairdresser, so that I could stop this from happening to others.

Your True Hairy Godmother

The responsibility of a stylist is not only to create a great style for the client, but to offer a great salon experience. There are times where I have been called upon to fix a bad haircut or color. I see the client's familiar anguish in the mirror, and it reminds me of my own. It's heartbreaking when I see the damage that has been caused to the hair but even more so to the hair trauma victim. I realize that I cannot heal the hair in one session, but I can help heal the person living with it.

I can give them the emotional support they need, an open ear to listen, and the promise that I will work hard to bring their hair back to health. It will just take some time.

When a client's anguish has been acknowledged, they leave the salon with hope, a sense of peace, and the realization that they have found a person who cares not only about their hair, but about their feelings as well. It is not the character of a true Hairy Godmother to slander or badmouth another stylist or salon. A Hairy Godmother should discourage criticism by seeking the best case scenario in all situations. The focus should remain on empowering others and offering inspiring and hopeful solutions. This is the role of a true Hairy Godmother.

Clients have shared countless stories of bad spells and hocus pocus in the salon, but not all are sad. There are strange and very funny stories. As time goes on, we are often able to laugh and learn from our past experiences. My client Barb shared the following story.

Dark Barb, the Sorcerer and Orange Hair

Barb is a current client of mine, not to mention one of the liveliest and funniest people I know. She is easy work with, and I enjoy her accounts of the things she experiences in life. She is a naturally pretty woman in her late forties, who doesn't need makeup, and wears just a touch of mascara. I was highlighting her dark, shiny hair on a busy morning, when I must have seemed a little distracted. Barb got a little nervous and with an alarmed voice she said, "Whatever you do, don't make me orange! I don't want orange hair!" I reassured her that she was safe, and as it turned out, she was. That was when Barb shared a bad spell experience she once had in a salon, when she went out of town just a few years ago.

She was getting highlights when something went terribly wrong. Barb recalled that she was told there was a problem with the product and her highlights came out bright orange! Barb had a friend seated in the chair next to her, in this swanky out-of-town salon. Her friend's eyes widened as she observed Barb's hair in horror. With raised eyebrows, she caught Barb's eyes, shook her head and quietly mouthed, "Oh, Barb. You're not going to like this. You're really not going to like this."

Barb's animated male stylist responded with reassurance, in his rich European accent, and said that once she got used to it, she would love it! He declared that she was so gorgeous; she was absolutely destined to meet the man she would marry, and all in the very next two weeks! Barb was not encouraged by the news, and so the stylist, in an attempt to compensate, offered a free makeup session (that she didn't need), and a $20 discount off the botched highlighting service. Barb reluctantly agreed to the makeup. "They applied heavy, sticky makeup all over my face, and it felt so yucky," she told me. "They also painted a bunch of black stuff around my eyes." She continued, "Whatever that stuff was, it would not come off easily. It took two days to completely get rid of all that black gunk."

Barb said she felt ridiculous walking through town with her new look. She felt like people were staring at her black raccoon eyes and bright orange hair.

Years later, Barb is able to laugh it off. "There must have been some weird magic, or even a spell in what he said," she told me, "because a couple of weeks later I was at a party, and I did indeed meet the man I was going to marry." It was a Halloween party, and so she believes that it was her crazy-colored hair that drew him over to her. She and her husband still laugh about her wild orange hair. I love Barb's funny stories.

Barb has experienced hair struggles that many women have dealt with, especially in their late forties and fifties. Here is another one of her stories:

Barb is known to me "Dark Barb" because one day, she shared an account of her journey through menopause, and how she recognized her alter-ego, which she referred to as Dark Barb. This was a demonized version of herself that would appear out of nowhere and wreak havoc on her life. She described it as the female version of the Incredible Hulk. In fact, Barb said she could be feeling just fine at one moment, and that in a literal hot flash — and after one glass of wine — she could feel Dark Barb moving in. She would look at her husband who would say, "She's here again, isn't she?" And Barb would reply, "Yeah, I think so. I think she's taking over. I'm pretty sure it's her again."

Menopause is another major factor when it comes to trauma in the salon chair. Hormones and emotional instability in general drastically affect the salon experience. Often these emotions aren't even related to the hair. Like Dark Barb, we never know when it's going to hit us. Even though we are aware it's happening, when we're in the moment and so full of emotion it's hard to discern what is really charging our emotions and causing us to react in a certain way. Is our perception based on fact or hormones? It's all about our perspective, which changes constantly.

Damsels in Distress

There have been princesses who have enjoyed the security and trust of their Hairy Godmother for years. Things seem to have a magic flow, and then suddenly, without any warning, a bad spell is cast and the magic becomes dark and scary. I can tell the minute someone walks into my salon when something is amiss. Even if it is their first visit, I can sense the anxiety, as the client's eyes scan the salon, looking around for warning signs, like nervous children checking under the bed for monsters.

Many frustrated clients are so disappointed by past hair experiences that they become locked in, and hyper-focused on what they don't want. This causes a loss in clarity of what they *do* want.

A compounding problem in cases like these, is that the consultation becomes almost a consoling session instead of a solution-seeking opportunity. Hairstylists get overwhelmed, and have no idea how to navigate to the solution. It is difficult especially when the clock is ticking, and the client appears alarmed — sometimes to the point where she is almost inconsolable. It's like dating someone fresh out of a bad break up who is focused on the bad experience and on what went wrong; except in this case, you have been hired to fix the heartache. I add extra time on the schedule for trauma cases, especially in the consultation. There is little or no chance of resolving situations like these without allotting enough time. Trust must be established before real healing can occur.

Sometimes we think things are worse than they really are. Our perception of problems is determined by our vantage point in life, and our emotional responses may change at any given time. Clients show different levels of panic and despair, especially when they're facing unpleasant results at the salon.

Our personalities are major factors in our response to critical thinking. Automatic and initial responses are formed by our personal history, genetics, social background and experience. If we're coming from a bad place, we tend to expect bad things. Do you know someone who has suffered a betrayal or a breakup, and then meets a nice guy, only to chase him away with the horror stories of the ex? The emotional scars and residual anger from the previous relationship hinder the possibilities for something better. They bring the old stuff in to the new relationship, which prevents anything good from happening.

The same can happen when a hair stylist confronts a hair trauma victim. I've experienced this dynamic with a number clients over the years. These clients have been traumatized by previous hairdressers, and so they come in with anxieties and hair horror stories that I have to disarm before we can even begin to identify any potential solutions.

The best thing stylists can do is to listen and to acknowledge the client's distress. Minimizing or deflecting the trauma only compounds the problem, and makes the client feel even worse.

Tara's Tale

Back in the 1990s, Tara was a young girl graduating from high school. She had very fine, long hair. Hairdressers would continually cut her thin hair too short when she went in for a trim, because it wasn't healthy. Tara avoided haircuts whenever she could, which made the ends even more fragile. The ends would split, fraying from the ends up, just like a rope.

I often see cases similar to Tara's in the salon. Each time it got stringy, she would surrender to her frayed ends. She went to a hairstylist who would see that it wasn't growing anymore; too much would be cut it off, and so the cycle repeated. This frustrated Tara, and she felt very vulnerable and ill at ease each time she entered the salon.

I recognized this on her first visit with me, and I promised Tara that I wouldn't cut as little hair as possible. I offered her a hand mirror and positioned her so that she could see the reflection of the back of her hair, in the larger station mirror. I would discuss what I felt needed, placing my comb horizontally and suggesting various lengths and options from which Tara could choose. Above all else, I wanted my client to feel empowered in the process. I would stay within her requested length, and snip the ends while she held the mirror and watched me. I would make eye contact with her and show her exactly what I was going to cut before I began. She would grant permission with a nod, and I would respect her wishes.

Over time, Tara began to trust me. She came in more often to get her hair cut, and gradually, her hair became healthier. Tara was very quiet and shy at first, but over time she grew more open. I became very fond of her as she worked her way through the college, by waiting tables in a local restaurant. I respected how hard she worked. When she graduated college, she became an accountant at an insurance company. And as her confidence grew in the world outside the salon, she acquired confidence in the salon chair.

One day, after about three years, Tara entered the salon with complete confidence, and opted for a Meg Ryan cut. This cut was very popular after the release of the movie *City of Angels*, starring Nicolas Cage and Meg Ryan.

This time, when I began cutting Tara's hair, my client and I discovered that her hair was in fact wavy and thick. The weight of her long hair had disguised her wave. With the short cut, Tara had transformed into a new person entirely. She looked and felt great.

Tara soon became my number-one referring client. I watched her grow from a young girl with terrible insecurities, into a confident and beautiful woman. I saw her get married, and then have a baby boy. Tara grew up into a very capable young woman. Ever since I gave her the Meg Ryan cut, Tara sat in my chair and trusted me to do whatever I thought was best. The days of her holding the hand mirror were far behind her. The spell was broken.

Roxanne's Chemical Cut and the Full Glass

Sometimes a phone call comes in, and we get notice of bad news. We may even be given the opportunity to prepare for an upcoming battle. I have seen some the bravest women I know face a dreaded cancer diagnosis, and with all of the dignity and grace of a royal. I do whatever I can to facilitate healing and support. My sisters in the industry are so compassionate and caring. We are hair nurses who help distressed patients manage the constant reminder of their sickness. I know hairdressers who have gone beyond the obligations of their job, all out of love and compassion for their clients. It becomes very personal to us in the industry, as we have all lost people to this terrible illness. We will wear both the professional and friendship hat in these crucial days.

Roxanne was a client of mine about fourteen years ago, from my first salon in Myrtle Beach, South Carolina. She was a married, beautiful mother of five, in her late thirties. She had been with me for about two years when she was diagnosed with breast cancer. Roxanne began chemo, and began facing the inevitable loss of her hair, but she decided to face the challenge head on and started to shop for wigs immediately

Roxanne called me, and I scheduled a private appointment for her after hours. She decided to confront the clippers and shave her head and tackle her hair loss on her own terms. She felt that she would be more empowered by choosing when to shave her head, rather than being stunned with a sudden hair loss in the shower clogging the drain or her golden locks left laying on her pillow case.

The appointment was set a week before she began chemo. She seemed fearless but I knew she was scared. Roxanne and I shared a very special time that evening, as we prepared to shave her head. It was just her, her husband Brian, and myself. He had brought in a special potion for his queen. He took a glass tumbler, already filled with ice, and added her favorite cocktail, Crown Royal and 7 Up. She sipped it while we talked. Then, when she was ready, I led her to the chair, draped her with a cape and took my clippers from my salon cart drawer. I began to shave her head.

It wasn't the first time I had to perform this task. In 1995, I did the same for my Auntie Edna, who had ovarian cancer. My heart felt just as heavy doing it for Roxanne. The truth is, that night Roxanne had to lead *me* through the process. I was afraid that I would shave too much too soon. She had a perfectly good head of shoulder-length hair at that point. I felt responsible for taking her healthy reflection and turning it into a symbol of cancer and visible illness. As hard as it was for me to shave Roxanne's head, I never lost sight of the fact that this was *her* fight. I needed to be strong and support her as she faced her battle. She was an absolute trooper. In fact, she had already selected great wigs to match the hair she was losing.

She had ordered some online, and found others through the local cancer society chapter. She was ready for the fight of her life.

Roxanne worked for a health insurance company, and planned to continue working as much as possible through her treatments. She was amazing. She kept a positive attitude, and even caused a hysterical scene in the salon, involving a shocking surprise for a little boy named Walker.

It was the end of another day, and Walker and his dad, Bob, had dropped by the salon. I was adjusting one of Roxanne's wigs while she still had it on. She was completely bald from the chemo at that point, but in great spirits. She did not look ill, and the wigs were so great that few people would notice she had cancer. Walker, however, liked to ask a lot of questions, especially while I was busy working.

He was a cute little fellow, and that night he just happened to ask, "Miss Michelle What happens if you make someone's hair fall out?"

Roxanne was seated in my salon chair. She didn't skip a beat, and suddenly she swung around to look directly at the boy and whipped her wig off, revealing her stunning bald head. She said, "See?"

Walker almost fell backward in shock, and then turned and ran outside to tell his dad, who had stepped out to make a phone call. We laughed hysterically as we watched Walker through the window, and heard him yell to his dad, who was still on the phone and looking very puzzled, as his seven-year-old son repeated, "Dad, Dad, that lady in there just lifted her hair clean off her head!"

It's been over a decade since she's had chemotherapy, and Roxanne is now in remission. Her family has grown larger and she now has beautiful grandchildren that she has been able to enjoy. I see her smiling pictures on Facebook, and feel joy in knowing that she has survived that terrifying time. However, she did more than survive it; she chose to thrive through it. Her Crown Royal and 7 Up was not the only glass kept half full, and I'm wondering if maybe there is some magic both.

The lessons learned through the darker times give us new insights. The lessons I've learned in the salon regarding bad spells and hocus pocus have taught me that we have a choice to always look for the best in any situation. We cannot change what happened in the past, but we can learn from it and apply our knowledge to make better choices in the present as well as the future.

Chapter 11

Real Magic and Better Spells

We have learned that the mirror's magic is closely related to the way we see ourselves. Our reflections are often marred by the dark spells of criticism, holding us captive, in the dungeons of negative self-talk. When we take time to focus on our strengths and qualities, your Hairy Godmother's magic becomes far more powerful. Negative thoughts are dark, while positive thoughts are light. Just as the night follows the day, they are always going to be present in our lives.

Your Hairy Godmother has to balance positivity and negativity, just as she does her acid and alkaline concoctions. The mixes she uses to transform your locks are filled with carefully calibrated colors and potions. Your Hairy Godmother has to know her craft and spells very well. She uses potions to balance the pH levels in your hair to keep you safe. The pH scale runs from 0-14 and you may have seen television commercials advertising shampoos that are specifically formulated to restore the hair's natural pH. Lemon juice, for example, has a low pH of 2.0 and is acidic. Hair lightening bleaches have a pH of 8.0 or higher, and are alkaline. Water is neutral at 7.0 I think that it is interesting to note that water is the essence of life, and it is perfectly balanced at 7.0, which is in the middle of the pH scale. Our opinions and views about ourselves, as well as others should maintain a similar balance to create the optimal environment for real magic to happen.

Communication is a vital component for your Hairy Godmother to bring it all together. This is the most difficult part of the magic to master. It's amazing how much time we spend looking directly at each other in the salon mirror, yet very often we don't recognize our *true* selves. The person we observe in the salon mirror is seated at the center stage. However, we must always be mindful that there is a much bigger story taking place beyond the castle walls. We often make assumptions about each one another, which can threaten the possibility for trust to form. This applies to both sides of the salon chair.

Clarity in the Cloud of Fairy Dust

Over the years, I've invested a great deal of time and money in psychotherapy and countless self-help books. At first, this journey was originally inspired, by my own failures and losses concerning personal relationships. Today, I am pleased to say that this heavy investment was absolutely worth it. I made remarkable self-discoveries in both my strengths and my weaknesses, and have developed new management skills along the way. As a result, I have applied the principles of this new self-awareness, both in my personal and professional relationships. I found that it has greatly improved the quality of communications when faced with adverse and tense situations.

At one point, I was known as "Princess Dark Cloud." This was due to a stream of tragic events that affected me, in a tsunami like fashion, and caused great emotional distress. Some of my greatest life lessons emerged from that dark cloud of despair, and have since inspired me to share them with those who seek to reach a higher self. It is important to remember that we are all in different stages of learning new wisdoms. We must keep in mind that it is very easy to get caught up in the excitement of our personal breakthroughs and inadvertently bombard others with these milestones. More often than not when learning from others, it is easier to digest new wisdom when searching at our own pace rather than have it thrust upon us. The starting point of positive sharing is respecting the boundaries of others. I have spent the last decade working to understand how my new clarity and approach to communication could heighten the standards of my work. I became a Certified Life Coach, and then applied the principles of active listening to salon consultations. I developed a systemized approach that clients and professionals have been eager to embrace.

HairCology™

When I started as a stylist, I did not *know* what I *did not know*. This is true of many of us in our careers as we mature and grow with experience. One of the greatest experiences of mine was becoming a life coach, because I was able to understand that what was happening in the chair was not just about the service, it was about the relationship. I began applying what I learned as a life coach to my work, and the results were amazing. I saw more smiles than ever, plenty of positive feedback and even more repeat business. Ultimately, through effective communication, and taking the time to really understand my clients' needs, I was able to transform my business, and never looked back.

The next step of the process was to share what I had learned with the world, because my goal was to reduce hair trauma all across the globe. This book was all part of the plan, as my intentions are to share my story and bring hope to those that have lost their way. I want to bring the love that I have experienced in my salon to others all over the world. There are many Hairy Godmothers in training out there, and so I knew I needed to develop a process that others could replicate. That was how my concept of HairCology was born. HairCology is the science behind client-stylist relationships.

I have created a certification program that teaches stylists how to coach and connect with their clients. As I said previously, this is not currently taught in Cosmetology School, but it is an essential component of positive experiences, and an award-winning service. Honestly, I cannot do it all from my humble salon in Hilton Head, South Carolina, and so I am bringing these techniques, and this certification program, to the rest of world.

One of the areas we really emphasize is the communication that takes place in the salon. We use the HAIR PIN method:

H- Hear what the client is saying by paraphrasing back to them

A- Acknowledge how they feel about what they are saying

I- Interpret the highest priority

R- Repeat back a summary and clarify the information they have shared

P- Prioritize the identified needs and select options for the client

I - Information is to be gathered and presented as concise options

N- Need to explain how the choices fit the priority and maintenance plan

S- Systematize, document and formulate plans; monitor results and updates.

This is the starting point of great communication both in and out of the salon. With our clients, a series of simple questions keep us on track. That way we can identify their core concerns and match them with the best options.

After actively listening to the client and identifying her priorities, we can then narrow the field to a maximum three possibilities. This helps the client become less overwhelmed with all her choices and saves time for the stylist.

We work hard to make sure that our stylists are using the techniques they learn in class. Catie Wolfe, who is my salon manager, and has been a top notch stylist in my salon for several years. She is my partner in a consulting company we founded to help stylists achieve their dreams. Catie has received accolades in her work using these communication principals. Since we began adopting these techniques, we've received plenty of feedback from online reviews:

> *I had a great experience at Chez Michelle during my short visit to Hilton Head. I was searching for a good salon to get my haircut, and I am so glad the internet brought me to this salon. Right from the off over the phone, they were friendly and accommodating to my schedule requests… surprising for a salon. I even walked in a bit early and was welcomed without having to wait. My stylist Catie was great! She was very knowledgeable and sweet, and helped me as an indecisive client who was not sure of what she wanted for a cut. Catie heard what I had to say and cut my hair perfectly. She even blew it out and styled it :)*
>
> *All of the ladies in the salon were fun and interesting. It didn't take more than 15 minutes for us to all be talking and laughing about life experiences over coffee and chocolate. I felt very much at home.*
>
> *I will definitely return on my next visit and would recommend to anyone looking for a good cut on Hilton Head!!!*
>
> *Betsy L. Bluffton, SC*

* * *

*My daughter was visiting from college and went
to a competing salon on Hilton Head Island for
foil highlights and a haircut, and the result was
horrible. I called Chez Michelle salon then next
morning to see what could be done to rectify
the poor job. Catie was able to meet with us to
review the problem and make a recommendation
for repairing the color. Catie spent almost 4
hours with my daughter to make sure that the
hair color and hair cut was fixed. She used
excellent products and was very patient and
worked tirelessly to make sure that we were
happy with the result. Very professional young
lady. I have booked appointments for myself and
my husband for next week! It's really nice to do
business with someone who is very competent at
their job and takes pride in their work.*

Theresa W. Hilton Head Island, SC

* * *

*Fabulous experience at Chez Michelle! I was
way overdue (6 months) for a cut and full
highlights. In Atlanta, I just can't find the time
to get my hair done! So, I decided while my
husband was available to "beach it" with the
kiddos, I would try a HHI salon! Michelle, the
owner, answered her phone after hours! They
booked me an appointment while I was on
vacation with Katie! Katie was wonderful and
my hair looks fabulous! I was a little nervous
since I had only done research on the web but
Katie did as wonderful of a job as my Atlanta
hairstylist! I will definitely go back as it's fun to*

*be pampered on vacation! I should also mention
that we didn't have conditioner in our condo
so Michelle and Katie even took care of me by
sending me home with a nice bottle of shampoo
and conditioner as a gift! Fantastic experience!
Thank you ladies!*

Lesley P. Atlanta, GA

* * *

*Made an appointment online and I was called
back within hours. I was scheduled for a haircut
within two days with Catie. I was a bit leery
as the owner was not available for 10 days but
Catie spent some time with me and we came
up with solutions to correct a bad haircut I had
received at home (NJ) It's a bit scary going to
a new hairdresser especially one so young. But
Catie proved to be very talented. I would highly
recommend this salon. They are personable
and well qualified. It is a small friendly
environment and owner operated. Michelle
is simply charming and my whole experience
was wonderful!*

Mary F. Belmar, NJ

We are committed to having everyone who walks
through our doors to feel like royalty, and for them
to feel heard. We want to help them feel better
about themselves, too. And now, we finally have the
opportunity to share this dream with other stylists and
bring a positive change to this industry.

Chapter 12

And They All Lived
Happily Ever After...

The magical stories and experiences that clients and hairdressers share can create connections so strong that they transcend the original client-service relationship. The unique friendships that begin in the styling chair extend far beyond the walls of the salon castle. Any hairdresser or client that has experienced this will describe it as one of the most trusted and valued relationships they have ever known. It is like having a family member who is occasionally woven into their personal and professional lives, and who becomes their ambassador and closest confidante, with a safe enough distance to offer the perfect combination of unconditional support and objectivity.

I have been blessed to experience more of these relationships than I can count, and they have helped define my definite purpose in life. Every client that has taken a seat in my salon chair has left an imprint in some special way. And to those of you I've disappointed, I would like to pay a special tribute to you as well. To those of you who disappeared into the abyss of those salon clients who didn't want to confront me or complain, I want to honor you now by letting you know that I am thankful for the lessons I've learned.

I wish you well, and hope that you have found a great salon home with a Hairy Godmother that treasures you. You deserve the very best service, and I am sorry I let you down.

I will close the final chapter of this book by sharing a few notes from my clients. I received these noted for my fiftieth birthday, as my salon manager, Catie Wolfe, was making a special memory jar for me. On the day the jar was presented to me, stuffed to the brim with notes, I read them one by one, and found myself sobbing uncontrollably. Every note was written proof, and validation, that what my clients and I share is real. It is love.

I was so surprised, and even though I can't share them all, I would like to share some of these notes, as I feel they reinforce the depth of clients' relationship with me, as *they* see it. I hope that I continue to grow and help more individuals see their true beauty—especially when they struggle to see it in their own reflection, just as I once did.

Kind Words from the Salon Castle

There are so many things I like about Michelle. I knew she was a special person the first time we met. My first hair appointment with her was a unique experience. I remember leaving there in a good mood. She has such positive energy and a spirit that can be contagious! I will never forget her singing and dancing that day. I thought, "This is a fun place!" That was almost five years ago. I have really learned a lot

*from Michelle, and she gives the best pep talks!
She always seems to know what to say to make
me feel better. I like that she is genuine and will
tell it like it is. I also admire her hard work and
that she loves to help others. She likes to keep it
moving and is always learning and doing new
things. I love that about her! Keep up the good
work, Michelle! You rock!!!*

Love, Marri

* * *

*I have been going to Michelle ever since
I moved to Hilton Head Island. She never
disappoints me when I get my hair styled. More
importantly, she is a good friend. Going to her
salon is like taking refuge from the storms that
sometimes occur in my life.*

Lori Dubiel

* * *

*You are such an upbeat, kind, and warm-hearted
person. You exude such a positive attitude and
outlook ALL the time, always looking for the
bright light rather than the dim. Michelle, you
have created such a wonderful atmosphere in
your salon that it is always a two-hour period of
time to which I look forward. You are so much
more than a hairdresser, my friend, you are just
that...my friend!*

Jodi W.

* * *

Michelle, I will never forget how much you have helped me through these hard times of grief since Tony died. You have been my rock! And I will never forget that you took time from your busy schedule to visit Tony at MUSC the day before he died.

Michelle, you are what true "friendship" is all about!

Love, Ellena

* * *

I remember meeting Michelle at Tara's many years ago. She changed my whole appearance that day. I walked in with dark hair and walked out a beautiful blonde.

My husband never stopped chasing me around the bed that night. Only kidding, but he loved the color and so did I. That was the beginning of my friendship with Michelle and I never looked back. She is one in a million with her great personality and that contagious laugh, which brings such joy to all who meet her.

Love, Mary Ann

* * *

I'm so glad God put you in my life for my hair, as well for my well-being. I can always count on you to make my day when I come in to see you. I love how you truly care about what's going on in my life. Michelle, to some you may just be a hairdresser, but to me, you're my shrink, my

*marriage counselor, my jester and my friend.
One of my favorite memories is when I was
having a day from hell, and you listened and let
me talk it out while I was trying not to cry. After
I was finished, I looked up at you and you just
smiled, then you said "Wow. I will make damn
sure that no matter what I won't mess up your
hair today.". It makes me laugh every time I
think about it. You are one of the truest people
I have ever known. Even when you're having a
day from hell, you still do great hair.*

Love Staci

* * *

*The first memory that I have of Michelle is from
when she was working in another salon, before
she opened her own. I was going to another
stylist at the time, and had been for years. I
couldn't help noticing what fun Michelle was
having at her station. Everyone she worked
on looked good. I didn't know her name. I was
visiting one day and noticed that she wasn't
there anymore. I asked the receptionist and
she told me Michelle had left. It took me a
long while to find her and I ended up going to
her salon in person, to be sure I could get an
appointment. What a fun lady!*

Gene, Hilton Head, SC

* * *

There is no one thing about Michelle that stands out alone, for she is so multidimensional. Aside from being loving, caring and giving, she is A LOT of fun and she makes me look beautiful!

Eliz

* * *

Back in the days of another salon, not too long after Michelle started taking care of my head ;-) she had a rather obstinate client who insisted on trying to take over my appointment ... and this woman was being very belligerent to sweet Michelle....

Well, ultimately (after some open-mouth amazement and a little discussion), Michelle and I decided she (the bad client) needed to be fired ... ironically, that's actually good memory !

It was a special twisted bonding moment lol.
Love, Mary Ann

* * *

You offer so much more than just wonderful hairstyling, although that is really important. The vibe you have created at the salon is so inviting, inclusive and fun! My favorite memory is the night we had dinner at Red Fish. It was a great evening of girl talk.

Thanks so much for being who you are!!
See you soon!
Lots of love, Jessica

* * *

Michelle has been an inspiration to me since the first day I met her. The positive energy she sends out when I walk in the door at the salon immediately puts me in a good place, and for the rest of the day a smile remains on my face.

Denise

* * *

My favorite memory is Michelle telling me she lost her bra at sea. I knew then we were going to be friends

Eileen

* * *

Michelle has the biggest and the kindest heart of anyone I know. I have had some pretty low times in the last three years, and she has always been there to pick me up and make me feel good about myself again. I know I can pick up the phone and call her, and she is always there, or if not at that exact moment, she will call me back! She not only is my hairdresser, but a very good friend. You deserve life's best, as you are a "GIVER," and God is looking down on you and smiling for the happiness you bring to others.

Love ya,
Sue

* * *

Michelle,

Every visit to your salon is a treat, and I always leave feeling better than when I arrived. You're a true professional, with high standards, great skills and a willingness to listen to your clients — for that we are devoted. I don't think many salon owners would be game to drag a chair outside on a beautiful, warm spring day and highlight a client's hair in the parking lot — but you seemed to enjoy the new territory as much as I did. It was a blast, although I think we did look odd to those passing by. Thanks for the memories.

Your staff and clients love you, and we all hope your humorous stories continue to entertain us for many, many years.

Thank you so very much for caring about us so much.
Love, Vicki

* * *

Dear Michelle,

I remember that at one of the first pool parties at the Preserve, you were dancing and singing. Everybody was laughing so hard because it was funny, but also because you were so good! I knew then that you would always be my friend because you are funny and entertaining!

Then you started doing my hair and I discovered that not only are you an excellent singer and dancer, but also an excellent hairdresser. I have really enjoyed being a part of your life, and you being a part of mine.

xoxo
Julie Roe

* * *

Michelle is a rare jewel! Where to start…?

Michelle, ma belle….

She can spin a tale, scissor cut and weave her magic …. pun intended … and have you at "LOVE IT" all through your salon appointment.

She makes you feel like you've been on a "Girls Day Out" and walked away looking fab, pampered, and refreshed, plus with a little "therapy banter" on both sides.

Don't get me wrong … she takes her color and cut very seriously!

My favorite stories … are the tales from the Island of No Return. You don't want to be colonized! Snap … OH, HELL NO.

Michelle speaks a unique language all her own … and if you are lucky enough to "get her" … no self-help books needed ….you are friends for life.

The "Happy Song" best describes Michelle's unique energy toward her craft, family of customers and on-going forever friendships!

Hugs … Laura P.

* * *

Dear Michelle

Your friendship has been one of the most important of my life. I feel that we were meant to meet, work together, spur each other on, and keep on doing so forever. You have been hugely influential to me … (sweeping circular motion with hands here) … and right at a time in my life when I despaired of anyone NEW coming along to affect me. Ha! Famous last words!

Our two years working together at Chez Michelle Salon were magical, don't you think? It was just goofy, funny, intense, beautiful, growth-filled, and I could go on and on. The "Charlie's Angels" photoshoot was wonderful, the Human Disco Ball was hilarious (and lives on in infamy!) … need I say more, my friend? And by the way, we saw each other through two engagements, two abandonments, and countless family foibles.

You are a special person and a survivor as well!

Leslie

About the Author

In the mid-eighties, at the tender age of 19, Michelle took a leap of faith, leaving behind her home town in Nottingham, England to venture across the "Big Pond" to America. She decided to pause her idea of becoming a history teacher in England, and instead try her luck at living the American dream.

Upon arrival, she almost instantly fell in love with the coastal living lifestyle on the shores of South Carolina and has lived there ever since. It has been 32 years since she made that 1st leap and she has never regretted it!

Once settled in America, Michelle re-called an earlier interest she had in the salon industry. This growing passion inevitably led her to become a hairdresser in 1990, at age 25. Once licensed, she began building her career and clientele in Myrtle Beach, South Carolina.

After only 3 years in the business, she opened her first salon, where she constantly sought to improve her skills as a hair care service provider.

In 2004, Michelle relocated to Hilton Head Island, to be with family, where she still resides today. She opened her 2nd salon in 2009, and celebrates the culture of a well-respected Paul Mitchell Focus Salon. Her hunger for learning still continued to fuel her desire for more education, not only in her own in her field, but in other areas as well. She expanded her communication skills by becoming a Certified Life Coach.

She shares her knowledge now as a Professional Speaker and Author, inspiring those around her with wisdom and humor. Michelle is passionate about effective communication as she believes it is the key to positive relationships both in business and personal environments.

She is a former National Educator and Certified Color Educator for John Paul Mitchell Systems. She teaches group classes for N.A.M.I (National Alliance for Mental Illness) and frequently speaks at various schools, businesses and events. Michelle has harnessed the power in reflective communication in the salon environment with both client and hairstylist relationships, with a particular focus on client consultation techniques. She recognized that many clients and stylists needed to develop consistent systematic and effective consultation dialogues, allowing freedom of expression for thoughts and ideas, preventing frequent misinterpretations.

Michelle partnered with her salon manager Catie Wolfe by forming StylistConsultLLC, a consulting company which facilitates HairCology™, Michelle's trademarked salon coaching programs certifies HairCologists™ who have mastered the principles of coaching consultations and communication techniques in the salon environment.

She has developed these systems and has enjoyed great success in her own businesses, and so is now committed to delivering these proven techniques to the salon industry and beyond. The benefits of these principles are huge in all aspects of personal and business communications.

For more information:

Updates and Purchasing Options:
www.YourHairyGodmother.com

Keynote Speaking Engagements email directly :
MichelleCaseySpeaks@gmail.com

Salon Coaching Classes go to:
www.StylistConsult.com

HairCology Certification Information:
www.haircology101.com

LinkedIn: Michelle Casey

Twitter: MichelleCspeaks@twitter.com